I0048914

Starting a Business

(3 books in 1)

The Complete Guide to Launch and Grow a Successful Business. Learn to Form LLCs & Make Business Plans. Master Market Research and Marketing Strategies

James Anderson

© Copyright 2023 - All rights reserved.

The content contained within this book may not be reproduced, duplicated or transmitted without direct written permission from the author or the publisher.

Under no circumstances will any blame or legal responsibility be held against the publisher, or author, for any damages, reparation, or monetary loss due to the information contained within this book, either directly or indirectly.

Legal Notice:

This book is copyright protected. It is only for personal use. You cannot amend, distribute, sell, use, quote or paraphrase any part, or the content within this book, without the consent of the author or publisher.

Disclaimer Notice:

Please note the information contained within this document is for educational and entertainment purposes only. All effort has been executed to present accurate, up to date, reliable, complete information. No warranties of any kind are declared or implied. Readers acknowledge that the author is not engaged in the rendering of legal, financial, medical or professional advice. The content within this book has been derived from various sources. Please consult a licensed professional before attempting any techniques outlined in this book.

By reading this document, the reader agrees that under no circumstances is the author responsible for any losses, direct or indirect, that are incurred as a result of the use of the information contained within this document, including, but not limited to, errors, omissions, or inaccuracies.

Table of Contents

Table of Contents

Complimentary Bookkeeping Guide

The Simple Guide to Bookkeeping eBook has been included which provides an introduction to bookkeeping and the different tools required. Bookkeeping is an essential part of business that is needed for tax purposes, regulatory compliance, and checking the financial health of your business.

To download, please scan the QR Code below or visit the link:

QR Code:

Link:
LindaHillBooks.com/bookkeeping

Book #1

A Beginners Guide to Properly Form and Manage an LLC.

Strategies to Maximize Asset Protection, Tax Breaks and Save Legal Fees

James Anderson

Introduction to This Beginners Guide for Forming a Limited Liability Company

Welcome reader, and thank you for picking up this book with everything you need to know to form an LLC in any state and protect your personal finances while maintaining federal tax advantages with the Internal Revenue Service.

Do you own a small business that is seeing an increase in revenue and looking into getting better organized for legal and tax purposes? Are you at the drawing board or in the business planning stage and ready to do your homework about LLC organization for your company?

Do you have an S-Corp or C-Corp company and want to legally reorganize to ease regulatory or tax burdens on your business? Are you a successful freelancer, social media influencer, or work from home creator of some kind and considering forming an LLC to separate your personal finances from your business?

This book is the ultimate and definitive guide to forming a Limited Liability Company for your business. Contained in its chapters is everything you need to know to start and maintain a Single Member LLC, a Multiple Member LLC, and specialized LLCs in certain states—such as non-profit LLCs or a Professional LLC for individuals or groups operating licensed businesses.

This well-informed, extremely up-to-date, and reader-friendly guide will also:

- Outline all the major business organization forms and explain their key differences for your business.

- Lay out the advantages and obligations of registering and maintaining your business as an LLC.

- And help you decide if an LLC is the right form for your business at the moment and later on down the road.

As the name LLC denotes, organizing your small business as a limited liability company combines the tax structure of Sole Proprietorships and Partnerships with the limited legal liability of a U.S. corporate organization like an S-Corp or C-Corp.

Millions of businesses in the United State find this to be an advantageous form of organization. It helps keep the liabilities of your business separate from your personal and household finances and liabilities. That protects you and your loved ones from any liabilities associated with the natural risks commercial endeavors are exposed to in the conduct of their business.

The LLC business form is appropriate and advantageous for all different kinds of businesses. Although this doesn't include every kind of business that might benefit from registering and operating as an LLC, the following is a list of businesses that can:

- Online businesses

- Brick and mortar businesses

- E-commerce, drop-shipment, Shopify, Amazon

- Uber and Lyft drivers, taxi, truck, and other drivers

- Social media influencers and content creators

- Retail and wholesale sales

- Import / Export businesses

- Skilled trades like plumbers, electricians, and home repair

- Home design and renovation businesses

- Wedding and event planners and caterers

- Restaurants and food businesses

- Chain franchise businesses of all kinds

- Freelancers and independent contractors of all kinds

- Independent consultants and sales reps

- Knowledge economy workers

- Data scientists, app companies, and tech startups

- And many other categories not listed here

LLC laws vary by state and there are different advantages and disadvantages to registering your company in different states. That is one of the cool things about LLCs is that you can register your business in any state regardless of the state you are operating out of.

So, you can shop around for the state whose business laws and civil courts suit your business best. This guide will go through the major differences state by state to help you pick the state that you like best to register your LLC.

Under state shield laws, owners and members of LLCs have limited or even no personal liability for the actions and debts of the company. In most U.S. states this legal and financial protection for individuals using the LLC organization is stronger than a corporate limited liability.

Meanwhile, limited liability companies enjoy more private regulatory control over their governance than corporations. That's why some businesses in the corporate weight class choose to remain large-sized "small businesses" with the limited liability organization, rather than commit themselves to the burdens of federal corporate regulatory compliance.

If you run a successful small business proprietorship or partnership that is growing annually in accounts or transactions or revenue, *the critical importance of this legal and financial shield for your personal and household finances cannot be overstated!*

Having that legal protection will not only secure your personal finances and peace of mind, it can also give you the confidence you need to scale your small business to the next level without worrying about taking on greater levels of personal financial and legal risk due to the potential liabilities when running any business.

This beginner's guide to LLC formation will teach you everything you need to know to start and maintain your company's LLC paperwork and status from start to finish.

In The Following Pages, You Will Learn:

Legal advantages and protections of forming an LLC

Record keeping and other obligations of your LLC and how to maintain them

Where to find the documents and forms you'll need to start an LLC and how to fill them out

Tax benefits and how to prepare your LLC's taxes

How to fund your LLC and manage its banking and finances

and the answer to every question anyone has ever asked about LLCs when deciding to form a limited liability company to protect themselves and their families from the legal and financial risks of running a business.

Before giving you all the information, you need to start and maintain your LLC, with the best, most up-to-date, and useful pointers for gaining the most benefits possible out of restructuring your form of business, this book will outline the difference between an LLC and other business forms like: Sole Proprietorships, Partnerships, S-Corps, and C-Corps.

That way you can know for sure if it's the right new form for your business. But first it's important to understand just how serious LLC protection is for you as you grow your small business. Then you'll see why there are so many LLCs in the United States today. By the year 2020, there were over 20 million registered LLCs in the United States according to IRS data.

The following true story, which played out in the United States District Court Southern District New York in 2016, is a harrowing example of why limited liability for companies became a form of business organization with important legal protections for business owners.

Why There Are Over 20 million LLCs in The United States

Unfortunately, the hero in our story was running his very successful YouTube channel business as an individual sole proprietor in his own name.

As a result, when another YouTuber filed an arguably frivolous lawsuit against the YouTube comedian, for making fun of the litigant's YouTube videos on his channel, all of his own personal finances and net worth were in danger of loss if he were to lose the court case.

At the time Ethan Klein was running one of the ten most highly subscribed channels on the platform, and in addition to becoming a global internet celebrity, with millions of fans in just a couple years of publishing one viral comedy hit after another, he had made a small personal fortune from the ad revenue from YouTube and affiliate commissions from his channel's sponsors.

Over the course of that year, Ethan and his shy wife, Hila, uploaded several videos to their popular channel, "h3h3productions," to keep their fans updated about the suit. They expressed in very emotional updates the crushing stress and anxiety of having everything they personally owned on the line in this court case.

If only they had taken a few days to learn the basics of starting a limited liability company and filed the paperwork and fee to register an LLC in a state of their choice!

A small amount of time to learn what he needed to know to protect himself and his wife from a business lawsuit that came out of nowhere would have certainly spared them both a lot of worries about their financial stability and future household security during this time.

No one plans for their business to deal with a frivolous lawsuit, a costly financial mistake, or a freak accident. The Kleins were surely floored that they could actually be sued for real, with actual danger of damage to their personal finances, all over some jokes posted to YouTube.

So, any kind of business, no matter how safe the owner may think their line of work is, can incur serious liabilities in the course of events.

When these unfortunate circumstances happen, they take business owners by surprise. But you can plan to be prepared for the unthinkable if it does happen, and set up your own household finances and legal liabilities separately from those of your business.

Mr. Klein said in one video update that going through this lawsuit was the hardest thing either he or his wife had to do in their entire lives. And Hila even served for a year in the army when she was growing up in Israel! Having to worry about losing everything they own is not something LLC owners have to live with, even in the event their LLC is sued for cause.

Fortunately for the Kleins, they did eventually win their case after 17 grueling months of stress and worry as they fought it out in court. The other YouTuber's claims of defamation and copyright infringement were both dismissed by the judge in what turned out to be a landmark ruling for digital fair use laws for creators online.

Let's put it in the same terms as limited liability companies. Sole proprietors and partners have *unlimited* liability as far as their business is liable legally or financially. Their position in the law and civil courts is one of being personally co-mingled with their businesses for all legal purposes.

While or after your business is being sued, if it doesn't have legal liability protections, you may not be able to get a loan for a home, refinance your home or take out a mortgage using your house as collateral, finance or lease a new vehicle, or lease office space your business needs to continue operating as you weather the legal process.

The U.S. is the most litigious country in the world, with a costly average of 40 million civil torts or lawsuits filed in the United States every year. A high population sample study conducted by the Small Business Association in 2014, found out of 65,000 small businesses, that every year a staggering range of 35% - 53% of small businesses are sued every year?

The good news is that LLCs are extremely easy to form and very easy to maintain, with a notoriously simple process and lots of flexibility in LLC statutes and case law.

In order to be sure if the organization is right for your business, the following chapter will outline and summarize the key important differences to your business between Sole Proprietorships, Partnerships, LLC structures, S corporations, and C corporations.

This guide will break down the differences in liability, regulation, and taxation among the different business types. Later chapters will describe LLCs in more detail, and teach you everything you need to know to maintain an LLC, prepare your federal tax filings, and pay your business' correct tax obligation on time each period to avoid IRS penalties.

CHAPTER 1

What Makes an LLC Different from A Sole Proprietorship, Partnership, S-Corp, or C-Corp?

I know a shoe maker who didn't start an LLC.
His business was a sole proprietorship.
I know an introverted entrepreneur in the coal industry.
He mined his own business.

In this chapter we're going to mind all our major business forms and you will learn about all the different major business structures out there and the key differences between a sole proprietorship, partnership, S corporation, C corporation, and a limited liability company or LLC.

On the Internal Revenue Service website's resource page for limited liability companies, which you can access by visiting the link underneath the quote below, the IRS defines an LLC thusly:

> *"A Limited Liability Company (LLC) is a business structure allowed by state statute. Each state may use different regulations, you should check with your state if you are interested in starting a Limited Liability Company."*

https://www.irs.gov/businesses/small-businesses-self-employed/limited-liability-company-llc

If you want to skip ahead to the chapter with state-by-state requirements for forming an LLC in each state, it contains a directory of resources to point you the right way so you can find the state office you need to send your paperwork to in order to register your LLC in that state.

But I recommend you read this chapter and the next first to make sure an LLC is really the right form for your business. Then Chapter 5 will go through different LLC laws and requirements state by state and lay out the advantages and disadvantages of filing your LLC in each one.

According To The IRS:

> *"Owners of an LLC are called members. Most states do not restrict ownership, so members may include individuals, corporations, other LLCs and foreign entities. There is no maximum number of members. Most states also permit 'single-member' LLCs, those having only one owner."*

Certain kinds of businesses are restricted from forming an LLC. Because of federal financial regulations, that includes most financial institutions like banks, financial trusts, and insurance companies.

Because of laws that vary by state, certain kinds of businesses are also restricted from forming an LLC in certain states. In California, for example, there are 93 different kinds of businesses that cannot be registered as an LLC. These include architects, accountants, and health care providers.

Still, other than these exceptions, which will be covered in greater detail in a later chapter, virtually any kind of sole proprietorship or partnership can file for LLC status to form a private limited company in a state of the members' choosing.

In addition to providing state legal and financial protection for business owners by separating them as private citizens from their businesses, the other main purpose of using an LLC form to register your business with the United States and file and pay your federal income taxes, is to maintain your sole proprietorship or partnership's pass-through taxation as a flow-through entity.

Pass-Through Taxation and Flow-Through Entities

Pass-through taxation is an accounting method for determining tax obligations. For business entities with pass-through taxation the IRS regards the income of the business and the income of the business' owner/operator or partners as one and the same income, so it is only taxed once.

C Corporations and Double Taxation

This way income from your business isn't taxed twice as in the case of companies incorporated as C corps, whose shareholders pay federal income tax on dividends and capital gains from selling shares, while another tax is assessed on corporate income separately from dividends.

The C corps income and the income of its shareholders are distinct taxable incomes and each is taxed independently of each other at their respective tax rates for the year.

They are considered by the tax code to be two distinct income streams for two different taxable entities (the corporation and each of its shareholders' individual income), and trigger two independent tax obligations that must be paid on each tax period.

LLCs, Sole Proprietorships, Partnerships, S Corps, And Pass-Through Taxation

Businesses that operate with pass-through taxation are called flow-through entities. They include sole proprietorships, partnerships, S corporations, and limited liability companies.

In each of these business forms, the company and its owners have one income, the same income, it's the income from the business, and the company's income triggers a single tax obligation for each income each tax period.

Sole Proprietorships, Partnerships, And LLCs Compared

So, when a sole proprietor files their taxes, they report income from their business quarterly as individual income tax using Schedule C on the individual tax return Form 1040. The instructions from the Internal Revenue Service for filling out Schedule C properly can be found here.

Sole proprietors can even use their own Social Security Number as the business' tax identification number. So, the business' income is the sole proprietor's individual income.

There is the caveat here that sole proprietors must also pay a self-employment tax in addition to their individual income tax rate for the amount of profit their business made for the year.

The business tax includes FICA taxes. FICA stands for the Federal Insurance Contributions Act. FICA taxes are your business' contributions to the U.S. Social Security and Medicare programs.

The sole proprietor's self-employed business tax also includes their contributions to state-administered federal unemployment benefits programs through FUTA and SUTA taxes, filed on the Internal Revenue Service's Form 940.

But with a sole proprietorship, the business' profits are not counted out as payroll to the sole proprietor, with an individual income tax obligation, and then counted against as corporate profits with an additional corporate income tax obligation added on.

With the rise of the Internet, e-commerce, social media influencers and creators, online courses and teaching platforms, and freelance work clearinghouses for a fast-growing segment of information work, there are more sole proprietors than ever before. As of the most recent counts, there are millions more sole proprietorships than there are limited liability companies.

Many of these sole proprietorships may be at a stage of maturity with their income and book of business that it is more appropriate for them to register as an LLC in a suitable state.

Forming An LLC Does Not Add to Your Tax Obligations If You're Starting with An S Corporation, Sole Proprietorship, Or Partnership.

Because an LLC is a flow-through entity, the taxation structure for your business will not have to change as a result of forming an LLC out of your sole proprietorship.

But you still get the limited liability protection from state shield laws for LLCs that will keep your legal and financial status secure against liabilities incurred by the operation of your business.

That's the advantage of starting an LLC vs. remaining a sole proprietorship or going ahead and starting out registering as one if you're all set to start transacting business on or soon after Day 1 of your new venture.

The difference between a limited liability company and a partnership is basically the same as the difference between an LLC and a sole proprietorship.

The difference is the number of members is more than one in a partnership or multi-member LLC, whereas the LLC "version of a sole proprietorship" so to speak, its analog among sole proprietorship businesses, is a single-member LLC.

But the pass-through taxation for all members of a multi-member LLC works the same as it did for their partnership.

So, by forming a multi-member limited liability company or limited liability partnership out of your existing partnership, you will not incur additional tax obligations to the federal government.

You also won't have an additional tax obligation waiting for your company's income if you start with a multi-member LLC instead of a partnership right out the gate for a new venture.

Like An LLC, S Corporations Have Pass-Through Taxation as A Flow-Through Tax Entity and Limited Liability for Owners' Personal Assets. Unlike An LLC, S Corporations Have More State Requirements and Strict Rules to Follow for How to Pay Shareholders.

According to the U.S. Internal Revenue Service's web page on S corporations:

"S corporations are corporations that elect to pass corporate income, losses, deductions, and credits through to their shareholders for federal tax purposes. Shareholders of S corporations report the flow-through of income and losses on their personal tax returns and are assessed tax at their individual income tax rates. This allows S corporations to avoid double taxation on the corporate income."

Now when an S corporation files its taxes, it reports income from its business quarterly as pass-through income to the corporation's shareholders.

S corporations can have only one class of shares and not more than 100 owners. Taxes are then assessed on the owners' individual incomes with the owners' deductions and at the rates of their individual income tax brackets corporations file their federal income taxes using the IRS Form 1120-S, and use Forms 941 and 940 for employment taxes. This includes FICA and unemployment taxes to contribute to the Social Security, Medicare, and federal unemployment benefits funds.

Individual shareholders then report their share of individual income from the S crop using the IRS Form 1040 and Schedule E, as well as other forms referenced on the S crop shareholder's Schedule K-1.

Income from S corps can also be paid out in the form of salary and dividend payments in ways that are advantageous for reducing the owners' tax obligation. Talk to a tax preparation professional or do your own research carefully to make sure you file your company's taxes properly.

S corporations also shield their shareholders' personal financial assets from the company's legal liabilities, whether they arise through lawsuits or contractual financial obligations. They are similar to limited liability companies in this way.

Another way S corps are like LLCs is they are fairly easy to convert to a C corporation should the company move in that direction. The owners can simply elect to file under the IRS Code Subchapter C. In either case, the new C crop will have to file documents with its state of incorporation as well and comply with state incorporation laws and regulations.

There are however some disadvantages to electing for S crop status for some businesses. There are also strict eligibility requirements that will disqualify some companies from becoming S corps. Only individuals, certain trusts, and certain non-profits can be owners. There must be 100 or fewer owners. There can only be one class of company stock.

These restrictions do not apply to LLCs. So, depending on the status of the members/owners of the business, the number of them, and the equity structure of the company charter, an LLC may be the best option for a flow-through tax entity with limited liability protection.

Another restriction that S corporations must follow, but that does not apply to LLCs is that S corps must pay owners profits in the exact percentage of their percentage ownership of company shares. LLCs are allowed to pay members any way they decide.

So, if you are the only member of your LLC and bring on another member, you can distribute half of your shares to the new member, but pay them 25% of the limited liability company's earnings, and yourself 75% of earnings each period. That gives LLCs more flexibility to decide how to compensate members than S corporations have under their more rigid dividend rules.

S corporations will also find themselves with a handful of more obligations to meet state and federal requirements in corporate statutes and regulations. While you can shop by state for the state with the incorporation policies that best fit your company, like you can with an LLC, there are still more encumbrances for your business than what LLCs are required to keep up with.

Like An LLC, C Corporations Are Considered Separate Entities from Their Owners with Their Own Legal and Financial Liabilities. Unlike An LLC, C Corporations Have Double Taxation, A Number of Advantages to Scale, And A Number of Additional Requirements.

According to the U.S. Internal Revenue Service's web page on Forming a corporation:

"In forming a corporation, prospective shareholders exchange money, property, or both, for the corporation's capital stock. A corporation generally takes the same deductions as a sole proprietorship to figure its taxable income. A corporation can also take special deductions. For federal income tax purposes, a C corporation is recognized as a separate taxpaying entity. A corporation conducts business, realizes net income or loss, pays taxes and distributes profits to shareholders."

As explained earlier in the sections on pass-through taxation, flow-through entities, and double taxation, C corporations may be obligated to pay federal income taxes on corporate income, and shareholders of corporate stocks may also have separate federal income tax obligations triggered by dividends from their corporate equity or capital gains from selling shares.

Unlike S corporations, C corporations are permitted to have different classes of shares and there is no limit on the number of owners. That makes C corps ideal for companies that plan to scale to serve a mass market of customers, or high sales revenue growth using investor capital, or that plan to go public with an IPO (initial public offering) to be listed on stock exchanges.

Tech ventures, digital startups, dot coms, apps, fintech companies, software-as-a-service (SaaS) companies, and companies with business plans to raise large amounts of venture capital from investors to scale might find the benefits of a C crop form most advantageous.

If you start an LLC and want to change it to a C crop form later, it's not very difficult to do if it's appropriate for your business situation and your company is ready to incorporate.

This company file form is specifically available to meet the needs of those kinds of companies. The form is culturally and infrastructurally entrenched in venture capital circles, Silicon Valley, and Wall Street, with an overwhelming amount of support for the C crop form.

However, companies that do not plan fast paced growth funded by venture capital or angel investors, that are not designed to scale to serve a mass market, and that would prefer to pay less taxes on company income and distribute it to a smaller number of active members associated with the business might find the LLC file form more appropriate and a C crop too cumbersome.

C corporations have a number of additional federal obligations and requirements that vary from state to state. They must have boards of directors, executive officers, shareholders meetings, corporate minutes, and allow shareholders to vote on major corporate decisions.

CHAPTER 2

Should I Form an LLC For My Small Business?

After learning the key differences between LLCs and all the other major business file forms, if you are still not sure that an LLC is the right business form for your company, this chapter has some additional information about limited liability companies.

It includes a Frequently Asked Questions section about LLCs below, as well as a Crunch stop business questionnaire about your company that might help you narrow down the way to legally organize your business that best fits your company's and your personal needs.

Filing an LLC is hardly a hassle compared to personally facing a serious civil litigation for a liability arising from the operation of your business, with all of your personal belongings and potentially your entire savings in jeopardy of loss.

The paperwork is not too difficult to figure out how to fill out correctly for just about any business owner who has managed to successfully grow a business to the point that registering an LLC would be the most prudent course of action. This book will guide you through that step by step.

Chapters 7 and 8 of this book will walk you through the steps of forming an LLC, maintaining it according to your LLC's state requirements, and paying your company's federal income tax obligation correctly. By the time you have finished reading Chapter 5, you should have a better idea of what state will work best for you to register your LLC.

But just in case you're leaning toward going from an unshielded sole proprietorship or partnership form to an LLC, only you're feeling hesitant about the hassle, the paperwork, creating any additional burdens for your business, or making any kind of major change

Please read on to learn about some more real stories of business owners who didn't file an LLC, but later on, became personally liable for the liabilities of their company.

Although they didn't believe they needed an LLC for their business at first, they later wished they had protected their personal finances from any liabilities arising because of their business.

Recently a law firm from South Dakota reported the 2018 case of a resident and business owner living in Sioux Falls who fell victim to what he and his lawyer thought was a frivolous lawsuit.

Travis owned a custom jewelry business that made special keepsakes and souvenir jewelry with custom logos, designs, and messages on them.

One day while he was enjoying a basketball game with his family, he got a frantic phone call from an employee. His business was being sued and he was being sued personally along with it.

Travis' company had recently fulfilled an order from a manufacturing company based out of Minnesota. The company wanted them to put their name and slogan on a set of watches.

This is common for companies that want to get a nice gift for their customers or employees. But apparently, a manufacturer in Florida had the same company slogan, but also had it trademarked.

The mousehole sued both the manufacturer in Minnesota that did not own the trademark, and sued Travis' business for putting it on the watches.

Travis and his company had no idea the slogan its customer ordered was trademarked. They most likely didn't know either. There's no telling how it even got around to the company in Florida.

But regardless his business had infringed a trademark. Unfortunately, he had not registered his company as an LLC, so his personal savings and property were on the line along with the business.

After spending months getting hammered by legal fees, he was finally able to settle the lawsuit by paying a large sum to the litigant in the case, the Florida manufacturing company.

He had to sell his Ford F-150 truck and his fishing boat to pay for part of the settlement. If only he had registered his business as an LLC, any liabilities arising from the operation of his business would have stopped at his front door.

Then at least he would have had the assurance that his personal property, cash, and savings couldn't be taken from him in the lawsuit.

If you've never been through one, ask someone who has. A lawsuit is one of the most exhausting and emotionally draining experiences that could happen to you. If you run a successful and growing business, it's absolutely right for you and your business to keep it separated legally from your household finances.

Another example that illustrates the importance of legal liability for business owners is the case of Luis, who owned an independent contracting company in Illinois that installed satellite dishes for DISH Network. He operated it as a sole proprietorship instead of as an LLC.

The company had installed a dish at a restaurant, but the employee mistakenly designated the address as a residential address instead of a commercial venue.

As a result, when the restaurant broadcast a boxing event and only paid the residential fee instead of the commercial rate, Garden City Boxing Club, the copyright holder to the broadcast, was deprived of a substantial sum it was entitled to by contract.

The commercial rate for broadcasts of its material in public venues was $20 times the maximum occupancy of the building where the event was streamed.

Because an employee working for Luis' dish installation business checked the wrong box on a form, the establishment streamed the event without paying the commercial rate.

Instead of suing the restaurant for the money it was contractually entitled to for the broadcast, the copyright holder chose to sue the contracting company because it was the installer who made the error causing its financial damages.

Even though it was the restaurant that got the benefit of the broadcast by adding value for its customers, and even though it was an employee who made the error, not Luis, and even if it was an honest mistake, now because Luis had not registered as an LLC, his own personal assets were at stake in the lawsuit.

Not only did he lose the lawsuit, but the judge granted the copyright holder a summary judgment, meaning the judge agreed the facts of the case were so well established and substantial, that the court automatically handed the litigant a win without even hearing Luis' counter arguments at trial.

If only Luis had devoted a little time each day for a week or two while keeping his business running, to learning about LLCs and how to register one in a state of his choice to protect his personal finances from the risks of operating a business.

Then he would have been able to shelter his company's income from corporate double taxation with a pass-through entity form as well as limit his personal liability in the event that the unforeseen should occur as it in fact did to Luis and his business.

Should I Form an LLC FAQ And Questionnaire

Do I Need an LLC To Start a Business?

No, of course, registering an LLC is not a requirement to start a business in the United States. You can start a business by filing for an S corporation or C corporation.

You also have the option of drawing up the agreement paperwork to start a partnership to do business with one or more business partners.

You can also do business as a sole proprietor without filling out any paperwork at all, by just transacting business and reporting your income to pay any tax obligations due on it.

Should I Start an LLC If I Already Have a Sole Proprietorship or Partnership?

There are trade-offs for every business form and the company founder or business owner is free to choose the company file form that they think is most appropriate and advantageous for everything under the balance of their care in their lives and business.

Will An LLC Really Protect My Car, House, And Other Personal Valuables?

LLC laws encourage entrepreneurship and small business ownership because they expressly safeguard individuals and households from the business' financial and legal risks.

In the event a company you own in whole or in part ends up owing substantial financial damages to be enforced by law, or even footing a huge bill to prevent that result at trial in civil court, if the company is organized as an LLC, the owners personal finances are strictly separated from those of the business by state shield laws that offer strong protection for business owners so that starting or owning a business in the United States is not any riskier than it has to be.

What Is the Cost of Forming An LLC?

To begin with, in most states the cost of time and effort to form an LLC is trivial if it's probably a good idea for your business. This guide will help you navigate quickly through the options with all the key differences that might matter to you. LLCs are designed to be easy on the business owner and their families if they have one, and easy for the business owner to start.

Are There Any Disadvantages to Forming An LLC?

Forming and maintaining an LLC will likely cost more in paperwork fees than maintaining a sole proprietorship. The state you choose to register your LLC will require a fee to file your paperwork and there are different maintenance and reporting fees for LLCs that vary from state to state. That's the main disadvantage of limited liability companies against sole proprietorships.

There are also additional paperwork refiling requirements for LLCs to transfer ownership shares among members or to new members. These will differ in some ways from transferring shares in partnerships and S corporations by state, but on balance the amount of time and hassle will be similar. Whereas for a C corporation it is easy to transfer shares. They are optimized for that very purpose among others from the pre-seed stage all the way to publicly traded companies.

Are There Any Other Benefits of Forming An LLC?

Forming a limited liability company has other benefits in addition to state shield laws for your personal finances. There's the flexible pass-through entity taxation referenced a few times earlier in this guide. All of the tax implications of forming your LLC will be ironed out in detail in Chapter 6.

There is also more flexibility and leeway for LLCs than other business forms with more cumbersome requirements. For example, LLCs do not have an obligation to hold annual shareholder meetings, have a board of directors, or keep up other administrative and paperwork obligations than S corporations and C corporations have.

Should I start an LLC for my side hustle?

It might not be a bad idea to start an LLC for your side hustle for any and all of the same reasons you might form a limited liability company for your full-time small business or startup venture.

Even if you only transact $500 a month in business with your side hustle, your business activities could expose your personal finances to civil actions against your side hustle business with no limits to your personal liability for remuneration to the litigant should they prevail in court.

Your personal cash, wealth, and assets could be seized by the court to pay for the litigant's compensatory damages, punitive damages set by the court, and even the litigant's attorney fees and the court's fees.

Should I Start an LLC As an Independent Contractor?

If you're an independent contractor operating as a sole proprietorship, your personal finances are vulnerable to any liabilities arising from your business activities to fulfill contracts.

Even if the work you are doing is contract work for hire, the client, the businesses the client serves with your contract work, or even some other unforeseen third party affected in some way by the operation of the business could bring a suit against you with all your personal belongings and assets at stake should their case against you prevail in court.

Should I Start an LLC For My YouTube Channel, Instagram, TikTok, Or Other social media That Is Earning an Income from Donations, Ads, And Sponsorships?

Even if you don't think of yourself as "in business," if you are earning any income from ad revenue, affiliate programs, sponsorships, merchandising, donations, or otherwise as a content creator with a website, blog, or social media channel, you are still engaging in commerce.

When making any money online or on social media, you are exposing yourself to the risks of a lawsuit in the event that your activities result in a third party believing they have a rightful claim to sue you in court for causing them some kind of harm addressable by a civil tort.

If you register an LLC for your business however, your personal finances are protected by state shield laws from lawsuits, frivolous lawsuits, debt collections, and other adverse legal and financial liabilities that could accrue to the business. A detailed summary of the advantages and disadvantages of LLCs for online businesses is the subject of the next chapter.

CHAPTER 3

Advantages and Disadvantages of LLCs for Online Businesses

Today there are not only more online businesses than ever before, but the pace of online business growth in the United States and all over the world is absolutely staggering.

According to EIG, the Economic Innovation Group:

"Nearly 5.4 million applications were filed to form new businesses in 2021 — the most of any year on record, based on the latest data from Census Bureau's Business Formation Statistics."

Total U.S. business applications in 2021 surpassed the prior year's new applications by one million. Meanwhile there were 3.5 million new business applications in the United States in 2019, and an average of around 2.5 million per year over the preceding decade.

So, 2021's growth in total new business applications signals exponential growth in entrepreneurship and new business formation in the United States. Much of that new business growth is directly correlated to the explosive growth in online users and online commerce.

According to IBIS World, 10% of total business transactions were conducted online. That percentage grew in a steady trendline for two straight decades to 28% of all business in 2023. We now live in a world where nearly a third of all business is conducted online.

Odds are good your business operates with the extensive use of the Internet. All your customers, clients, followers, fans, marketing, advertising, inventory, communications, and admin may be entirely online.

As of Q4 2020, Forbes reported that two million YouTube, Instagram, and Twitch creators make an annual six figure income from ad revenue, affiliate marketing, merchandising, donations, and other income streams from their YouTube channels.

Millions and millions of online businesses are extremely lucrative for their owner/operators and the primary source of their personal income, so they make their livelihoods from their online business. It's important for online business owners who are having success with their business to protect their personal and household finances from the business' liabilities. Luckily, it's relatively easy and U.S. business law is designed that way.

It's Relatively Easy to Start and Maintain an LLC In Most States.

The LLC business file form was originally designed with the ease and convenience of the business owner in mind as well as their legal and financial safety.

Over the past fifty years, states have adopted limited liability and state shield laws to encourage residents to start businesses and bring their ideas and products to market.

The basic requirements to form an LLC from state to state are starting by choosing a name for your LLC. Rules for company names differ some from state to state. Your LLC's name may have to say "LLC" or "Limited Liability Company" at the end of it.

As long as it meets your state's requirements, you can pick whatever name you like for your business. It does not have to be the same as the name of your brand, channel, product, or your name if you operate as an online business or influencer using your legal first and last name.

After picking your company's name, you then file the LLC paperwork with your state's filing office usually with the secretary of state.

They have different names for it in different states like articles of organization or certificate of organization, but regardless of the state's official term for it, it's just some paperwork to let them know you have an LLC and give them your contact information.

Most states require that you list a "registered agent" who can receive paperwork on behalf of your LLC in case the state wants to send you a summons or notice of any suits or court enforced debt collections. Don't panic. That can be you. You just give them your address on the paperwork to form your LLC.

The Limited Liability Protections of State Shield Laws for LLCs Are Great for Online Businesses.

As in the case of Ethan Klein and "h3h3productions" told at the beginning of this guide, online businesses are not immune to the same risks of liability that conventional brick and mortar businesses are.

Even if your business dropships products and doesn't manufacture them yourself, any liabilities arising from one of your customers' uses of the product could result in a lawsuit for your business as well as that of the manufacturer.

If your business sells digital information products and a customer believes that taking action based on information, they used in your product caused harm to them or their business, even if you published accurate information in a responsible way, you could find your online business in a lawsuit.

There is no entirely risk-free way of doing business in an imperfect world and online businesses are no less vulnerable to these risks because of the greater separation the business owner has from all the business' contacts from behind the keyboard. LLCs help make these risks fair and acceptable so business owners can confidently manage and grow their businesses.

LLCs Have Tax Benefits That Are Probably Ideal for Most Online Small to Medium Businesses.

If you're an online business owner considering forming an LLC, odds are good you currently operate as a sole proprietorship and pay taxes as individual income for a self-employed individual sole proprietor, or similarly operate a partnership with a business partner.

Unless you are a tech startup with a business or app looking to scale and sell to another business or make your shares available on stock exchanges with an IPO or public listing, your online business probably pretty neatly fits the mold of sole proprietorships or partnerships as a pass-through entity for tax purposes. LLC makes it easy to keep this tax status while keeping your business and personal accounts legally separate.

There Are Some Additional State Tax and Fee Obligations for LLCs.

If you choose to register an LLC for your business, you will incur some fees and possibly additional state tax obligations depending on the state you select to incorporate your LLC.

State corporate rates range anywhere from 1% to as high as 9.99% in the Commonwealth of Pennsylvania. The states of Wyoming and South Dakota have no state income tax for LLCs or corporations.

Various states have differing rules for LLCs and some of them impose more burdens and obligations on business owners who register an LLC than others. These can include additional fees and costs paid for at the expense of the business owner to keep their LLC compliant.

Although operating a business in any of these states under a sole proprietorship, partnership, or other corporate form may incur similar costs, fees, and state tax obligations.

Your LLC could cost you more time and money than a sole proprietorship.

While the advantages of an LLC are hard to overstate, not every business owner who has registered one was happy about the experience.

Not all of the LLC "horror stories" where an LLC ended up costing the business owner time and money are from the same states, but they do tend to turn up more in states with more complicated and onerous LLC rules like California, New York State, and Alabama.

Chapter 5 of this guide will go over the main differences in LLC laws among the different states, and provide you with a state-by-state guide to help you pick the state that suits the needs of you and your business best to register an LLC.

Some of the ways LLCs could result in undesired results for your business include registering in a state with a high corporate and individual income tax rate, in a state with high property taxes, or in a state with onerous and costly rules for transferring shares or property to or from your business.

In one notorious case of an LLC filing gone sour, reported by the OC Register in December 2019, a California business owner wanted to sell some commercial real estate he owned for decades.

The only problem was his LLC bought it more than 30 years prior, then he let the LLC's registration lapse for 33 years. To sell the property, he had to pay 33 years' worth of filing fees and late fees to reactivate the sleeping LLC, cutting into his profits from the sale.

FAQ: Is an LLC Right for My Online Small Business or Social Media Business?

The number of new online businesses has boomed over the last twenty years, but we are seeing an absolute explosion of new businesses in this decade.

Not only are a vast number of these businesses enabled and powered by the platforms that connect us over the Internet, but they were not even possible or conceivable just a mere few years ago.

A social media channel creator who reviews extremely rare items for a very niche community, a single dad who drives his kids around with him to find used books in his city to buy and sell for retail prices on Amazon, an art student who draws graphic designs and illustrations for small business websites and some big corporate clients too— all of these can yield a lifetime of good earnings for the entrepreneurs that put in the research, planning, time, and effort.

If you have an online business that is beginning to see some major growth, or you already depend mostly or entirely on it for your income and livelihood, now is the time to seriously consider what kind of official business file form will serve your situation best.

Here are some questions that might help you make that determination for yourself:

How Much Revenue Is Your Business Earning and How Fast Is It Growing?

The lowest LLC filing fee in the United States is currently in Arkansas ($45 online with a required $150 annual "Franchise Tax Report") and the highest LLC filing fee is in Massachusetts ($500 to file with a recurring annual $500 renewal fee). In 2023 most states charge something like a $100 filing fee to register your LLC +/- around $50.

Does your online business earn more annually than the average amount of state filing and renewal fees for an LLC? If you earn about the amount of the filing fee annually, then filing for an LLC would lead your online business to break even on revenue if you have no other expenses.

In that case it may not be worth it to you unless you prioritize limited liability for your commercial endeavors before profits. Once your online business begins to average the amount of the filing fee in the state you would pick to register on a monthly basis, then it might be time to get serious about protecting your household finances so your business can grow with adequate legal protections in place.

Although it will eat into some of your profits up front, limited personal liability for your business fundamentally changes your mental calculus, and you might find your business grows much faster after registering an LLC than before, so that it doesn't actually eat into your profits, but becomes an important factor in their sustainable growth.

Would You Like to Give Yourself A 20% Tax Deduction on Your Federal Income Taxes Through 2025?

Do you feel like you pay too much in federal income taxes already? This is one of the greatest advantages of forming an LLC in the United

States, at least through 2025 when this extremely generous tax deduction sunsets if it is not renewed.

What if instead of donating to a politician who promises to cut taxes, writing an anti-tax letter to the editor, and going out to a tax protest, all you had to do to give yourself a 20% tax cut was fill out some paperwork and throw them a $100 filing fee?

In 2018 the Tax Cuts and Jobs Act, a major tax overhaul, took effect and created a tax deduction for owners of pass-through entity businesses like LLCs.

Pass-through business owners who qualify under the TCJA can deduct up to 20% of their LLC's profit after expenses from their income taxes. In other words, you pay taxes on 80% of what you brought home instead of on all of it and get 20% of your income tax free.

If you didn't know about this before and haven't taken advantage of this, please run the numbers on your business and see how much sense it makes for you. The tax cut is available through the 2025 tax year and will expire on Jan 1, 2016 unless it is renewed by an act of Congress.

Depending on your online business' earnings, the filing and renewal fees for an LLC are trivial compared to this tax cut. Simply registering an LLC can be like giving yourself a significant raise by simply filling out the paperwork and sending it to your state's registry office for LLCs.

Do You Have Plans to Grow and Scale Your Online Business?

If your online business is in the initial stages, but you have plans to grow and scale it into a full-time or significant part-time business, go ahead and complete this guide to forming LLCs so you will have all the information you need when your business operations begin to scale.

Have You Made Plans to Grow and Scale Your Business but Stalled, Delayed, Or Failed Repeatedly?

There are a number of reasons why new businesses stall, delay, or fail to grow in line with the entrepreneur's hopes or expectations. A lack of sufficient time and effort put into a profitable business plan is one.

A business plan that is not profitable regardless of the time or effort put into it— because of insufficient profit margins, an addressable market that is not large enough to support a business, inadequate quality for the product or even the advertising and marketing— is another.

There could be any number of specific causes for these reasons that businesses fail to launch in the individual case history of any business and its principals. Please allow me to suggest one possible cause here that may not naturally occur for most entrepreneurs to consider.

It could be that you have a viable business plan, but that you haven't put as much force behind it as it requires to be successful as you're defining success for your business. It may also be that the reason for this is you do not have enough confidence in the business.

For whatever the reasons, averseness to the costs and risks as well as insufficient confidence in the incentives of putting in more effort to increase the business's key numbers, one way to increase your confidence with a substantial improvement to the risk profile of your business that you can rely on is to register an LLC.

How Much and What Kind of Risk Does Your Business Take on In Its Operations?

Doing a simple risk assessment of your business is no replacement for professional consulting and legal advice, but it can help you to err on the side of being more conservative if you would like to minimize your liabilities from conducting business.

There are some questions you can ask yourself to get a sense of the risks involved in your business and whether registering an LLC might be a worthwhile investment for your household and business.

How many customers does your company transact business with on a regular basis? And what is the average revenue from each customer?

The larger your book of business grows with more clients, and the greater the sums involved in your business' transactions, the greater your exposure to the risks of a business lawsuit against your company.

At some point as your business scales, registering with a U.S. state and officially participating in its legal systems and protections will not just be advantageous but basically a necessity. Incorporation or limited liability registry is essentially a legally and financially hygienic standard of proper business organization in the United States.

What Kind of Work Does Your Business Do?

The more products or services your business offers, and the greater the complexity of those products and services, the greater your business' exposure to all kinds of risks of lawsuits, regulatory enforcement actions, financial liabilities, and other liabilities.

Even if you do not consider your business to be very high risk, unfortunately, business owners that get tangled up in issues that leave them liable without state protection are often blindsided by them, and consider them to be the most random and unfair matters to get into trouble over.

Does Your Business Employ Anyone or Plan to In the Near Future?

It's not only your business' customers or some unforeseen third party affected in some way by the downstream effects of your business' activities that might endanger your household finances by filing a lawsuit against your unprotected business.

Company employees can and do sue business owners every year. Even hiring freelance contract workers exposes your business to the potential risk of a lawsuit from one of them in the course of doing business.

As you hire more employees or contractors to fulfill your customers' orders, you also increase the risk that some action taken by one of them leaves your business liable in a civil action. In any event, if your business is registered as an LLC, the liabilities are limited to the assets of the business and your personal finances are safe.

CHAPTER 4

Difference in LLCs By State and How to Choose the State to Register Your LLC

The state you choose to register an LLC will have differing requirements and advantages from other states. Some states are generally more favorable to small businesses than others in their tax policy and commercial regulations. Fortunately, you are allowed to pick out the state you would like to register your LLC in even if you do not live there or primarily operate there.

In order to help you choose the best state for your business to register as an LLC, this chapter will provide you with highlights of the best six states to form an LLC, the worst five states to form an LLC, five acceptably good states to form an LLC, and a list of all the current LLC filing and renewal fees by state. But first, here's a brief history of the origins of the LLC business file form in one innovative state and how it spread to become a business file form standard in all 50 U.S. states.

History of LLCs

If you are a small business owner living in the United States in the 21st century, you are incredibly fortunate for a great number of reasons! One of them is that you have the limited liability company file form available to protect yourself and the ones you love from the risks and liabilities that arise in the natural course of operating a successful business.

Business owners in the United States didn't always have such strong protections to encourage and incentivize them to take more risks in the healthy sense of growing a small business legally, ethically, and practically to fill a need in the economy and earn profits from the business.

The limited liability company came into existence for the very first time in 1977 in Wyoming. The Hamilton Brothers Oil Company successfully lobbied the Wyoming legislature to get the same tax benefits and liability advantages in Wyoming that it had while operating in Panama.

The bill to enact limited liability protections for businesses operating under the LLC form was particularly crafty. It was designed to carve out these protections for state businesses that registered as LLCs within a framework that was compliant with Internal Revenue Service Kanter (1960) regulations to determine the method of federal business income taxation for businesses.

However other states were slow to adopt this business form because they were uncertain whether the IRS would find it valid, or take enforcement actions against their states' businesses and create a bureaucratic nightmare and costly surprises for business owners.

Then when the IRS explicitly ruled in 1988, in Revenue Ruling 88-76, that Wyoming LLCs were taxable as pass-through entities like partnerships, it unleashed a wave of state adoption of their own versions of the Wyoming LLC law. From 1992 through 1997, a wave of 40 of the 51 U.S. jurisdictions that have LLC statutes today passed their first LLC laws.

Since then, the body of case law for LLCs has grown dramatically, so that the business environment for LLCs is even safer and more predictable now than it was when the LLC file form was a novel business form.

Why You Can Register Your Business as An LLC In Any State from Any State

State LLC laws allow businesses that operate in other states to register as out-of-state LLCs. Usually, you have to get a Certificate of Authority from the other state by filing some application paperwork and a small filing fee similar to the fee to register your LLC.

Because LLC laws allow for out-of-state businesses to register, and because state laws don't prohibit businesses from registering as an LLC in another state, you can register your business as an LLC in any state from any state.

If you have substantial operations in your home state however and register out of state, you may be required to pay taxes in both states.

That would increase your business' tax burden, so it's worth going over your home state's "Nexus" laws carefully to find out whether your business operations in-state are considered substantial enough by statutory standards to meet the threshold for "Nexus" and trigger tax obligations in your state.

Generally having a physical presence like a storefront location, employees in your home state, agents or representatives that operate in your state, and/or a certain number of sales to customers or clients in your state will meet the threshold for Nexus.

Best Six States to Form an LLC And Why

Wyoming - Wyoming has the lowest tax rates for businesses of any state in the union. The State of Wyoming has zero personal taxes and zero corporate taxes. You pay 0% business income tax to the State of Wyoming on your limited liability company registered in Wyoming.

That's one of the main reasons why it tops this list for best states to form an LLC, but it's not the only reason. Wyoming is the state that originally invented the LLC and has especially strong protections for limited liability companies and a pro-business environment throughout the state.

South Dakota - South Dakota is another state with zero personal taxes and zero corporate taxes due in the State of South Dakota. That's why it ranks next on this list of the best six states to form an LLC in the United States.

Like Wyoming, that's foundational to South Dakota's strategy to attract businesses to the state. South Dakota is like Wyoming in its innovative approach to limited liability law and periodic retooling of its LLC policy to make life easier for businesses in South Dakota.

Though if your business has employees, you may be obligated to pay a reemployment assistance tax. See the page on this at the South Dakota Department of Labor & Regulation: https://dlr.sd.gov/ra/businesses/default.aspx

Texas - Texas is another ideal state to register an LLC tax-wise because it has zero personal income tax. So with your limited liability company organized as a pass through entity with your personal income and your business income counted as the same income for tax purposes, you will owe zero income taxes to the State of Texas for your LLC registered there.

Texas' corporate income tax is also very low. The Lone Star State charges a Gross Receipts Tax of 1% on corporate gross income above $1,000,000 annually. So, it is a very favorable tax environment for LLCs and a very pro-business state.

Texas also has more LLCs registered than any other state in the union. So, Texas also has the most case law and legal precedent for disputes involving LLCs. As a result, it is a more predictable environment for LLCs to operate. Finally, Texas is one of the few states with provisions for Series LLCs. This LLC form allows business owners to register multiple LLCs owned by a single LLC all for the same fee structure as registering one LLC. This is advantageous for business owners with various real estate holdings to keep their liabilities separate so that the liability of one property does not extend to the others.

Florida - The Sunshine State also makes it onto this list of best states to form an LLC because of its zero-tax rate on personal income and corporate tax rate of 5.5%.

That's a very favorable tax environment for your limited liability company when there are states with tax rates as high as 9% and 11% for LLCs to pay.

Florida allows business owners to elect to form their LLC as a pass-through entity with state taxes on personal income (zero), or to organize as a corporation and pay the State of Florida's corporate tax rate of 5.5%.

LLCs in Florida are also loosely regulated with regard to business ownership structure. Businesses can easily register in Florida as Single-Member LLCs, Multi-Member LLCs managed by multiple owners, and Multi-Member LLCs managed by a manager that the owners appoint by an organized method in their charter.

Delaware - While the State of Delaware may not have as many LLCs registered as Texas, there are still over a million corporations in Delaware based all over the United States.

Delaware corporate policy is such a gold standard for business that half of all publicly traded companies and 64% of all Fortune 500 companies. The State of Delaware has a Division of Corporations that works to help new startups that incorporate in the state.

Delaware has a "General Corporation and Business Entity Law," to exempt them from some out of state income taxes. Delaware's initial filing fees are low, it has low franchise fees, and its corporate law has strong protections built in for the privacy of business owners.

Delaware is such a pro-business state that it created its Chancery Court for business disputes to fast-track dispute resolution. Delaware's expansive case history for corporate law is a standard used by courts across the United States for reference when deciding aces in other states.

Nevada - The Tax Foundation's Business Tax Climate Index ranks Nevada fifth in the nation as far as favorable taxes for businesses.

Nevada is another state on this list of best states to form an LLC because of the state's zero taxes on personal income and zero taxes on corporate income. Additionally, because of the handsome revenues from Nevada's tourism and gaming industry, Nevada has no state admissions tax, estate tax, gift tax, unitary tax, franchise tax, nor inventory tax.

Nevada is another one of the few states that allow for Series LLC formation through its limited liability company statutes. Also leave it to Nevada to have expedited levels of LLC approval so that you can get an LLC registered with the Silver State in under an hour.

Worst Five States to Form an LLC and Why

California - The Golden State's entire tax structure is based on the reality of how many ultra-wealthy businesses and residents live there. As a result, its taxes are debilitating for small and new businesses. California ranks 25th in the nation in state corporate tax rates, and it ranks near the very bottom at 49th for the individual income tax rank.

California has a low filing fee for limited liability companies of $70, however its annual renewal fee for LLCs is a whopping $800. That's the highest annual renewal rate for LLCs in the union. It's far more than the $500 renewal fee for Massachusetts LLCs and more than twice as much as the five states that have $300 or $350 renewal fees for limited liability   companies.

Connecticut - If you register your LLC in Connecticut, your business will be on the hook for higher state taxes as well. The Nutmeg State has a state corporate tax rate of 7.5% and a state personal income tax on 3 - 5% of your reportable income.

It ranks 27th in the nation on corporate taxes, and Connecticut and near last with California with a state individual income tax ranking of 44th in the union. Commercial property is also very expensive in Connecticut, and the state ranks dead last in 50th place among the states for its high property taxes.

Louisiana - Louisiana is another state with high taxes that aren't favorable for the growth of small to medium sized businesses. You may want to consider avoiding registering in LLC to save your business' profits from the Bayou State's 4 - 8% state corporate tax rates and its 2 - 6% tax rates on reportable personal income in the state.

Louisiana ranks 35th among U.S. states on corporate tax rates and 32nd among U.S. states on personal income tax rates. Louisiana also ranks 49th on state sales taxes.

Additionally, Louisiana courts and case law are peculiar and more rigid than laws in other states, having their influence from the Napoleonic Code rather than the English common law systems that have worked so well for businesses in states like Delaware and Wyoming.

Vermont - Yet another state to avoid over its taxes if you can when picking out one to register your LLC is Vermont. The Green Mountain State ranks 44th among U.S. states on state corporate tax rates and it ranks 39th in the union on state individual income tax rates.

The state corporate tax rates in Vermont are 6 - 8.5% and the state personal income tax rates are 3.55 - 9.4%. Vermont also has very high property taxes, ranking 49th out of all states in the union on personal property taxes. This is a major disadvantage for any business that uses commercial space.

New Jersey - The last state on this list of five worst U.S. to form an LLC is New Jersey, because of its relatively high state corporate and individual income tax rates. The Garden State ranks 48th in the nation on state corporate income taxes and dead last at 50th among all U.S.

states on state personal income taxes.

New Jersey has state corporate tax rates ranging from 6.5 - 9% and state individual income tax rates ranging from 1.4 - 10.75%. Corporate tax rates in the state have recently improved only marginally, and the tax relief was offset by hikes to New Jersey's state unemployment insurance taxes.

Five Acceptably Good States to Form an LLC and Why

Alaska - Alaska ranks middle of the road on state corporate taxes at 26th in the nation, but it ranks the very best out of all U.S. states on personal income taxes. That's why it ranks on this list of five acceptably good states to form an LLC.

The Last Frontier State has state corporate tax rates ranging from 2 - 9.4%, and zero state taxes on individual personal income for your limited liability company registered in the state of Alaska. The State of Alaska does not collect a state sales tax either.

Montana - Montana is another middle of the road state as far as forming an LLC. It ranks out of all U.S. states 21st in state corporate tax rates and 25th in state individual income tax rates.

The Treasure State has a state corporate tax rate of 6.25% and state personal income tax rates of 1 - 6.9%. Montana's greatest strength taxwise is its low state sales tax constitutionally limited to 4%. That ranks Montana 3rd out of all states in the union on state sales tax rates.

New Hampshire - While the Granite State ranks out of all fifty states 41st on state corporate tax rates, pretty low on the list, it ranks 9th on state personal income tax rates. That's why New Hampshire is on this list of acceptably good states to form an LLC.

The State of New Hampshire has a state corporate tax rate of 8.5% and a state individual income tax of 5%. With no state sales tax as well, New Hampshire has a very tax friendly environment for small to medium businesses.

Indiana - Indiana is a solid upper-middle tier state to form an LLC in on the basis of the tax advantages in the state. The Hoosier State ranks 12th in the nation for state corporate tax rates and 15th in the nation for state personal income tax rates.

The State of Indiana levies a tax at a rate of 8.5% on corporate income in the state and 3.4% on individual income in the state. Indiana also has no requirements for LLCs to hold regular meetings and keep minutes, but must file a business entity report every 2 years.

Utah - Out of all states in the union, Utah is another good upper-middle-tier state in terms of state limited liability company statutes and case law. The Beehive State ranks 14th out of all U.S. states on state corporate tax rates and 10th in the union on state individual income taxes.

That's why Utah rounds out this list of five acceptably good states in which to form a limited liability company. The State of Utah has a state corporate income tax rate of 5% and a state personal income tax rate of 5%.

Utah is a very pro-small business state with a friendly startup environment. Eligible LLCs in the state can apply to the Utah Governor's Office of Economic Development for corporate incentives for Utah LLCs. Utah also offers microloans up to $50,000 for qualifying LLCs in the state to help capitalize small businesses through the Utah Micro Loan Fund.

Current LLC Filing and Renewal Fee Schedule by State (2023)

(Table organized in alphabetical order.)

- **Alabama** LLC Filing Fee $200, LLC Renewal Fee $100 (yearly)

- **Alaska** LLC Filing Fee $250, LLC Renewal Fee $100 (every other year)

- **Arizona** LLC Filing Fee $50, LLC Renewal Fee $0

- **Arkansas** LLC Filing Fee $45, LLC Renewal Fee $150 (yearly)

- **California** LLC $70 ($0 until June 2023!), LLC Renewal Fee $800 (yearly + $20 every other year)

- **Colorado** LLC Filing Fee $50, LLC Renewal Fee $10 (yearly)

- **Connecticut** LLC Filing Fee $50, LLC Renewal Fee $80 (yearly)

- **Delaware** LLC Filing Fee $90, LLC Renewal Fee $300 (yearly)

- **Florida** LLC Filing Fee $125, LLC Renewal Fee $138.75 (yearly)

- **Georgia** LLC Filing Fee $100, LLC Renewal Fee $50 (every other year)

- **Hawaii** LLC Filing Fee $50, LLC Renewal Fee $15 (yearly)

- **Idaho** LLC Filing Fee $100, LLC Renewal Fee $0

- **Illinois** LLC Filing Fee $150, LLC Renewal Fee $75 (yearly)

- **Indiana** LLC Filing Fee $95, LLC Renewal Fee $31 (every other year)

- **Iowa** LLC Filing Fee $50, LLC Renewal Fee $30 (every other year)

- **Kansas** LLC Filing Fee $160, LLC Renewal Fee $50 (yearly)

- **Kentucky** LLC Filing Fee $40, LLC Renewal Fee $15 (yearly)

- **Louisiana** LLC $100, LLC Renewal Fee $35 (yearly)

- **Maine** LLC Filing Fee $175, LLC Renewal Fee $85 (yearly)

- **Maryland** LLC Filing Fee $100, LLC Renewal Fee $300 (yearly)

- **Massachusetts** LLC Filing Fee $500, LLC Renewal Fee $500 (yearly)

- **Michigan** LLC Filing Fee $50, LLC Renewal Fee $25 (yearly)

- **Minnesota** LLC Filing Fee $155, LLC Renewal Fee $0

- **Missouri** LLC Filing Fee $50, LLC Renewal Fee $0

- **Montana** LLC Filing Fee $35, LLC Renewal Fee $20 (yearly)

- **Nebraska** LLC Filing Fee $105, LLC Renewal Fee $13 (every other year)

- **Nevada** LLC Filing Fee $425, LLC Renewal Fee $350 (yearly)

- **New Hampshire** LLC Filing Fee $100, LLC Renewal Fee $100 (yearly)

- **New Jersey** LLC Filing Fee $125, LLC Renewal Fee $75

- **New Mexico** LLC Filing Fee $50, LLC Renewal Fee $0,

- **New York** LLC Filing Fee $200, LLC Renewal Fee $9 (every other year)

- **North Carolina** LLC Filing Fee $125 LLC Renewal Fee $200 (yearly)

- **North Dakota** $135 LLC Filing Fee, LLC Renewal Fee $50 (yearly)

- **Ohio** LLC Filing Fee $99, LLC Renewal Fee $0

- **Oklahoma** LLC Filing Fee $100, LLC Renewal Fee $25 (yearly)

- **Oregon** LLC Filing Fee $100, LLC Renewal Fee $100 (yearly)

- **Pennsylvania** LLC Filing Fee $125, LLC Renewal Fee $70 (every 10 years)

- **Rhode Island** LLC Filing Fee $150, LLC Renewal Fee $50 (yearly)

- **South Carolina** LLC Filing Fee $110, LLC Renewal Fee $0

- **South Dakota** LLC Filing Fee $150, LLC Renewal Fee $50 (yearly)

- **Tennessee** LLC Filing Fee $300, LLC Renewal Fee $300 (yearly)

- **Texas** LLC Filing Fee $300, LLC Renewal Fee $0 (for most LLCs)

- **Utah** LLC Filing Fee $54, LLC Renewal Fee $18 (yearly)

- **Vermont** LLC Filing Fee $125, LLC Renewal Fee $35 (yearly)

- **Virginia** LLC Filing Fee $100, LLC Renewal Fee $50 (yearly)

- **Washington** State LLC Filing Fee $200, LLC Renewal Fee $60 (yearly)

- **Washington DC** LLC Filing Fee $99, LLC Renewal Fee $300 (every other year)

- **West Virginia** LLC Filing Fee $100, LLC Renewal Fee $25 (yearly)

- **Wisconsin** LLC Filing Fee $130, LLC Renewal Fee $25

- **Wyoming** LLC Filing Fee $100, LLC Renewal Fee $60 (yearly)

CHAPTER 5

U.S. IRS Tax Advantages and Obligations for an LLC

After registering your LLC with a state of your choosing you will be responsible for filing regular income reports to the U.S. Internal Revenue Service (IRS) and paying any federal tax obligations owed from your limited liability company's profits.

LLC Is a State Designation Not a Federal or IRS Category.

Limited Liability Companies are a business file form sponsored, registered, and regulated by state LLC laws. They are not a federal or IRS designation or category of business. The IRS understands they exist, but doesn't have very much in the way of special rules for LLCs.

(Although there is a huge federal tax deduction for LLCs through 2025 by an act of Congress. It will sunset in 2025 unless it is renewed by another act of congress.)

Here's what the IRS has to say about LLCs as a business classification on its LLCs page:

"Depending on elections made by the LLC and the number of members, the IRS will treat an LLC as either a corporation, partnership, or as part of the LLC's owner's tax return (a "disregarded entity").

"Specifically, a domestic LLC with at least two members is classified as a partnership for federal income tax purposes unless it files Form 8832 and affirmatively elects to be treated as a corporation.

https://www.irs.gov/forms-pubs/about-form-8832

"For income tax purposes, an LLC with only one member is treated as an entity disregarded as separate from its owner, unless it files Form 8832 and elects to be treated as a corporation. However, for purposes of employment tax and certain excise taxes, an LLC with only one member is still considered a separate entity."

https://www.irs.gov/businesses/small-businesses-self-employed/limited-liability-company-llc

LLC Owners/Members Can File Income Taxes As:

- A Sole Proprietorship

- A Partnership

- A Corporation

Here's how the IRS defines a Sole Proprietorship:

> *"A sole proprietor is someone who owns an unincorporated business by himself or herself. However, if you are the sole member of a domestic limited liability company (LLC), you are not a sole proprietor if you elect to treat the LLC as a corporation."*

If your business is a single member LLC, then the IRS regards it as a "disregarded entity" and you can file your federal income taxes for your LLC as a sole proprietor.

To file and pay federal income taxes, self-employment tax, Social Security and Medicare taxes, federal unemployment tax, and excise taxes as a sole proprietor for your single member LLC business income, use:

1. 1040, U.S. Individual Income Tax Return
   https://www.irs.gov/forms-pubs/about-form-1040

2. Schedule C, Profit or Loss From Business
   https://www.irs.gov/forms-pubs/about-schedule-c-form-1040

3. Schedule SE (Form 1040 or 1040-SR), Self-Employment Tax
   https://www.irs.gov/forms-pubs/about-schedule-se-form-1040

4. 1040-ES, Estimated Tax for Individuals
   https://www.irs.gov/forms-pubs/about-form-1040-es

5. 941, Employer's Quarterly Federal Tax Return
   https://www.irs.gov/forms-pubs/about-form-941

6. 944, Employer's Annual Federal Tax Return

   https://www.irs.gov/forms-pubs/about-form-944

7. 940, Employer's Annual Federal Unemployment (FUTA) Tax Return

https://www.irs.gov/forms-pubs/about-form-940

If your business is a multi-member LLC, then the IRS classifies it as a partnership for federal income tax purposes, and you can file your company's taxes and pay any federal income tax obligations from your business' earnings using the following IRS forms:

1. Form 1065, U.S. Return of Partnership Income
   https://www.irs.gov/forms-pubs/about-form-1065

2. Form 941, Employer's Quarterly Federal Tax Return
   https://www.irs.gov/forms-pubs/about-form-941

3. Form 940, Employer's Annual Federal Unemployment (FUTA) Tax

Return
https://www.irs.gov/forms-pubs/about-form-940

Individuals in multi-member LLCs filing their federal income taxes as owners in a partnership can do so by using the following IRS forms:

1. Form 965-A, Individual Report of Net 965 Tax Liability
   https://www.irs.gov/forms-pubs/about-form-965-a

2. Schedule E (Form 1040), Supplemental Income and Loss
   https://www.irs.gov/forms-pubs/about-schedule-e-form-1040

3. Form 1040, U.S. Individual Income Tax Return
   https://www.irs.gov/forms-pubs/about-form-1040

4. Schedule SE (Form 1040), Self-Employment Tax
   https://www.irs.gov/forms-pubs/about-schedule-se-form-1040

5. Form 1040-ES, Estimated Tax for Individuals
   https://www.irs.gov/forms-pubs/about-form-1040-es

LLCs that elect to pay federal income taxes as corporations by filing the IRS Form 8832, can do so by using the following IRS forms:

1. 1120, U.S. Corporation Income Tax Return
   https://www.irs.gov/pub/irs-pdf/f1120.pdf

Instructions for Form 1120 U.S. Corporation Income Tax Return

https://www.irs.gov/pub/irs-pdf/i1120.pdf

2. 941, Employer's Quarterly Federal Tax Return
   https://www.irs.gov/pub/irs-pdf/f941.pdf
   Instructions for Form 941

https://www.irs.gov/pub/irs-pdf/i941.pdf

3. 940, Employer's Annual Federal Unemployment (FUTA) Tax Return

4. https://www.irs.gov/pub/irs-pdf/f940.pdf Instructions for Form 940https://www.irs.gov/pub/irs-pdf/i940.pdf

Qualifying LLCs Get a Federal Tax Deduction of 20% Through 2025.

The Tax Cuts and Jobs Act of 2017 gave eligible LLCs a 20% tax deduction on federal income taxes every year through 2025. Qualifying businesses can pay taxes on only 80% of the taxable income they earn for the year, an incredibly generous tax cut for the LLCs that qualify.

To qualify for the 20% tax deduction, the business must be a pass-through entity, and the business owner's income must not be more than $157,500 for the year for a taxpayer filing as single, or $315,000 a taxpayer's total household taxable income if married.

Some Other Ways to Give Yourself a Tax Cut and Save Money on Your Taxes

If you're not already maximizing all the opportunities to legally reduce your federal income tax obligation for your LLC and keep more of your business' earnings, here are some ideas to point you in the right direction. In addition to the 20% qualified business income tax deduction good through 2025, one of these could return a tidy sum of your LLC's profits each year:

Buy Health Insurance and Get a Tax Deduction

The IRS provides special tax exemptions for self-employed workers when they pay for their own health insurance policy. If you are self-employed for your LLC and buy your own health insurance policy, you might qualify to get the exemption.

LLC members or sole proprietors of an LLC (e.g. freelancers, independent contractors, and gig workers, among other self-employment type sole proprietors), who are unmarried or unable to obtain health insurance through the policy of a spouse, may be able to deduct some or the entire cost of their self-employment health insurance premiums from their taxes.

Save For Your Retirement in an IRS Tax Advantaged Savings Account

Professional financial advisors typically say that it is important for U.S. workers, whether you are employed or in business for yourself, to save at least 15% of your income over every income period for your retirement to ensure you will have enough retirement savings in addition to your social pensions benefits from Social Security to maintain the standard of living you have become accustomed to over your peak income earning years.

The U.S. tax code provides a number of long-term savings accounts and retirement accounts with very generous tax benefits to workers who regularly save some of their monthly income in these accounts for long term savings toward a large purchase or retirement savings.

Self Employed business owners registered as an LLC without any employees, for example, can start a single-participant 401(k) plan called a "Solo 401(k)," "Solo-k," "Uni-k," and "One-participant k." It has the same rules and requirements as any other 401(k) plan.

When you contribute money from your LLC's earnings to a 401k savings account for your retirement, you get to deduct the amount of your 401k contribution from your yearly taxable income obligation. You only pay taxes on money stashed into a 401k when you withdraw them. Ideally this is at a much later date when the money you saved on the deductions has had time to go to work for you to cover your taxes when you go to withdraw the funds. Over a lifetime, this can work out to some enormous, truly standard and quality of life changing amounts of money spared from taxation and allowed to stay in your control with your nest egg.

With a Roth IRA or Roth 401k account, you pay taxes when the money

57

goes into the account, but future withdrawals from the account are tax-free, so that if your money has had time to go to work for you, and accumulate some substantial capital gains, you get those gains tax free.

You will have to wait a certain amount of time to withdraw from a Roth IRA before the tax-free benefit kicks in. For the tax-free benefit, you will have to wait five years to withdraw (the IRS calls it making "distributions" to yourself from your Roth IRA or Roth 401k account), and you cannot withdraw the funds until you reach the age of 59 years and six months from your date of birth. Usually, Roth tax savings on contributions are somewhere on par with your tax bracket rate.

Maximize Your Federal Income Tax Deductions from Business Expenses, Your Car, Home Office, and Depreciation

Deduct Expenses from The Operation of Your Motor Vehicle

If you need to use your vehicle to drive for your business, you can get a tax deduction on your federal income taxes by keeping a record of either your mileage when driving your vehicle for work purposes related to your LLC, or by keeping records of your actual expenses to pay for gas, oil, maintenance, and repairs. You can also deduct vehicle expenses for tires, registration, vehicle fees, and taxes, as well as your lease or car payments and your car insurance.

All you have to do is log all your miles and categorize them for business or personal use. When you do this, imagine you have to explain in person to an IRS employee why you categorized mileage as a business expense and do the right thing and be honest to the best of your ability using common sense. Your percentage of business use is your percentage of vehicle costs that you can deduct from your federal income taxes for the year.

If you keep track of your mileage instead and use that to deduct business transportation costs from your taxes, simply log your miles and the standard mileage rate for tax deductions is $0.585/mile Jan 1 - Jun 30 and $0.625/mile Jul 1 -Dec 31.

Depreciation Expense Deduction for Property Your LLC Owns

Most small businesses including LLCs own equipment, tools, or devices that are essential to their operation. The IRS allows businesses to write off their decreasing value as they age due to normal wear and tear from use as a business expense called depreciation.

There is a wide variety of accounting methods used in the Generally Accepted Accounting Principles (GAAP) of the commercial sector to determine depreciation. The flexibility the IRS has with depreciation calculations is so that businesses can fairly and accurately calculate how the depreciation of their company's assets affects their balance sheet at the end of each year.

It is not so that taxpayers can shirk paying taxes by finding creative but inconsistent or even dishonest ways to account for their depreciation expenses. Do your research when exercising this tax savings benefit and make sure that you don't file any depreciation expenses for a tax reduction in your LLC's tax return that you couldn't justify to an IRS official speaking in person with them to explain how your arrived at the figures on your tax returns.

The most common and simplest way to calculate your depreciation expense for any property owned by your LLC (like your computer if mostly used for business, vehicle if mostly used for business, office equipment and supplies, machinery, or anything else your business owns and uses that wears out over time and needs to be replaced) -- is the straight-line method.

Using the straight-line method, you simply estimate when an item of business property will have to be discarded or sold at the end of its useful life and the most you can realistically expect to sell it for if anything. That is called the salvage value. Subtract that from the price on your receipt for purchasing the item, then divide by the number of years until the item is fully depreciated.

That figure is the depreciation expense that goes on your tax return for each year of the item's remaining usefulness until it is discarded or sold in order to get the tax reduction for it.

Hire an Income Tax Professional That Specializes in Tax Savings for LLCs and Small Businesses

If you've got more money than spare time to go into depth and learn all the tax savings that are available to LLCs like yours in the federal tax code, you may consider hiring an income tax professional that specializes in tax savings for LLCs and small businesses.

Professional tax preparation services or a CPA could help you find and unlock enormous tax savings for your business by making the required reports and filings with the IRS for your LLC's federal income taxes.

If you're still starting out and bootstrapping is more valuable to your business than saving time, there are a number of free and affordably priced tax preparation software services that might be able to help you identify and take advantage of tax relief that your business qualifies for.

Here are some of the top recommendations for small business tax accounting software, by some of the most trusted brands in financial and business news and advice:

Small Business Tax Software and App Recommendations

(These are not endorsements nor paid advertisements, and the author and publisher make no guarantees regarding the quality or results of the services, but you might find them worth reviewing.)

NerdWallet Recommends

NerdWallet recommends Intuit QuickBooks Online as the best in terms of **"overall accounting software"** for small businesses. It's very feature rich with a massive amount of app integrations and tools for businesses. The tradeoff though is a longer learning curve for a more robust software, and it's more expensive compared to the competition.

For freelancers NerdWallet recommends FreshBooks. The financial news and advice website likes FreshBooks because it is simple and affordable for freelancers with small businesses. They also mention the mobile app for FreshBooks as outstanding for freelancers operating on the go. If your company is fast growing and needs audit trails to share with accountants then it's not a workable solution.

https://www.nerdwallet.com/best/small-business/accounting-software

Forbes Advisor Recommends

For 2023 Forbes Advisor ranks the following tax software as best for small businesses: TaxSlayer Self-Employed, Intuit TurboTax Self-Employed, H&R Block Self-Employed, and Cash App Taxes.

Forbes recommends TaxSlayer as good for businesses with **complicated tax returns** and for its low filing fee of $100 (TurboTax's similar product is $170).

Forbes says TurboTax is the most expensive software it reviewed for the list with the link provided below, but that it's worth it for the **excellent customer service** and features like an IRS audit risk assessment.

Advisor also mentions H&R Block Self-Employed as another good tax filing option with a **budget advantage** over TurboTax, and Cash App Taxes as a reliable option for some of the minimum basics of tax filing for a business, but for **free and without many upsells** by CashApp.

https://www.forbes.com/advisor/taxes/best-tax-software-small-business/

CNBC Recommends

CNBC recommends Intuit TurboTax for its step-by-step guidance through the process of filing your taxes. TurboTax Live also provides advice for your questions instantly when you need it, and TurboTax will have a tax expert give your return a final review, prepare it, sign off on it, and file it with the IRS for you. TurboTax is CNBC's top recommendation for small business tax software for those reasons.

CNBC's runner-up tax software recommendation is H&R Block because of its simple, step-by-step guidance that's **easy to** use to file your taxes, unlimited chat or video support, over 11,000 physical locations so you can meet with a tax expert in person, and a support guarantee for free assistance if your business is audited by the IRS to help you know what to do.

For best free tax software for small businesses, CNBC recommends FreeTaxUSA with a federal filing software service that is free to use. It is a freemium model with optional upgrades, including a Deluxe edition with priority customer support, live chat, and audit defense in the event of an IRS audit.

Like the other recommendations on this list, FreeTaxUSA offers a maximum refund guarantee and 100% accuracy or your funds returned.

https://www.cnbc.com/select/best-tax-software-for-small-businesses/

CHAPTER 6

How to Form An LLC: State by State Requirements and Official Form Files

Before choosing a name for your LLC, be sure to type it in first (and maybe some close variations of it you can think of) into the U.S. Patent Office's Trademark Registry Database search engine so that you can be sure not to infringe on a registered trademark. If you use a registered marque, your business could be liable to civil action by the trademark owner. You can use the link provided to find the trademark database search:

https://www.uspto.gov/trademarks/search

Alabama

To register an LLC in Alabama, just file a form for a Domestic LLC if you reside and operate in the state or a Foreign LLC if you're out of state. Visit the Alabama Secretary of State's website at the link provided below for complete requirements and to file online.

https://www.sos.alabama.gov/business-entities/llcs

Alaska

To register an LLC in Alaska, visit the Alaska Department of Commerce, Community, and Economic Development's Division of

Corporations, Business, and Professional Licensing page for corporate forms and fees at the link provided below. Navigate to the Limited Liability Company Domestic (Alaskan) or Limited Liability Company Foreign (Non-Alaskan) page to register your in-state or out-of-state LLC.

https://www.commerce.alaska.gov/web/cbpl/Corporations/CorpFormsFe es.aspx

Arizona

To register an LLC in Arizona, visit the Arizona Corporation Commision's Corporations Division using the link provided below. Choose a name for your LLC, purchase a domain, check name availability with the ACC at http://ecorp.azcc.gov/ using File > Name > Check Name Availability. Then submit your formation documentation to register your LLC.

https://azcc.gov/corporations/ten-steps-to-starting-a-business-in-az

Arkansas

To register an LLC in Arkansas, visit the Arkansas Secretary of State's Business and Commercial Services page at the link provided below. Navigate to the link for a Domestic LLC or Foreign LLC as applicable to your business and follow the instructions.

https://www.sos.arkansas.gov/business-commercial-services-bcs/forms-fees/llc

California

To register an LLC in California, visit the California Secretary of State web page for Starting a Business and Business Entity Types for complete instructions for how to form a Limited Liability Company or Limited Liability Partnership in the State of California.

Then visit the California Secretary of State "bizfile Online" web page and register to create a secure online account, then follow the instructions on the California Secretary of State web page. The links for these official State of California pages are provided below.

As the California SoS notes, "an operating agreement among the members as to the affairs of the LLC and the conduct of its business is required."

https://www.sos.ca.gov/business-programs/business-entities/starting-business/types

https://bizfileonline.sos.ca.gov/

Colorado

To register an LLC in Colorado, visit the Colorado Secretary of State web page on limited liability company formation using the link provided below. The filing fee must be paid online.

Read and take into account all the information on the first page, and then click the "Next" button at the bottom of the page, and it will take you through a quick 11 step questionnaire to get all the information the Colorado state department needs to register your LLC there.

https://www.sos.state.co.us/pubs/business/helpFiles/LLCintro.html

Connecticut

To register an LLC in Connecticut, visit the Connecticut Business page for LLC forms using the link provided below. The Connecticut Department of State has a section for Domestic LLC forms and Foreign LLC forms. Use the Certificate of Organization and Application for Reservation of Name forms to register a Domestic LLC in the State of Connecticut. To register an out of state LLC, use the Foreign Registration Statement and Application for Registration of Name forms.

https://business.ct.gov/manage/all-business-filings/llc-forms?language=en_US

Delaware

To register an LLC in Delaware, visit the Delaware Division of Corporations web page for forming new business entities using the link provided below.

Business entities registered in Delaware are required to have a Delaware Registered Agent. You can choose from a list of Delaware Registered Agents at the link provided below.

https://corp.delaware.gov/agents/

https://corp.delaware.gov/howtoform/

Florida

To register an LLC in Florida, visit the Florida Division of Corporations page for limited liability companies, an official State of Florida website, using the link provided below. You can file online using your credit card to pay the LLC filing fee or print out a PDF from their website and fill it out by hand to mail in with the filing fee by check or money order.

https://dos.myflorida.com/sunbiz/forms/limited-liability-company/

Georgia

To register an LLC in Georgia, visit the LLC registration page at the official website of the State of Georgia at the link provided below. Whether you're an in-state or an out of state LLC you will have to find and choose a registered agent located in Georgia to receive service of process, documents, and any other official communications from the state of Georgia for your business.

https://georgia.gov/register-llc

Hawaii

To register an LLC in Hawaii, visit the business registration page for foreign limited liability companies if you are out of state and the one for domestic limited liability companies if you are in state. If you a registering a foreign limited liability company in Hawaii, you must file an Application for Certificate of Authority for Foreign Limited Liability Companies using Form FLLC-1 on the Hawaii page for foreign LLCs.

Foreign LLC: https://cca.hawaii.gov/breg/registration/fllc/
Domestic LLC: https://cca.hawaii.gov/breg/registration/dllc/

Idaho

To register an LLC in Idaho, visit the State of Idaho business website and Secretary of State's Office web page for business forms to file by paper with an additional $20 processing fee or find the link file the official Idaho forms to register your LLC online. You can use the links provided below to navigate to these pages. There are instructions on the business registration page to apply for an Idaho business license from a local municipal authority as well.

Business Registration: https://business.idaho.gov/register-a-business/

Business Forms: https://sos.idaho.gov/business-forms/

Illinois

To register an LLC in Illinois, visit the Office of the Secretary of State of Illinois' official website for LLC Articles of Organization guidelines and resources using the link provided below.

Please note that in addition to filing the required paperwork and paying the registration fees, LLC registrants in Illinois "must appoint and maintain a registered agent and registered office within the boundaries of Illinois. The agent is designated by the company as having authority to accept service of process." https://www.ilsos.gov/departments/business_services/organization/llc_instructions.html

Indiana

To register an LLC in Indiana, visit the State of Indiana's official page on starting a business using the link provided below. The State of Indiana's INBiz page will guide you through the steps to select your type of business, check business name availability, find a registered agent in the state who can receive legal and tax documents, as well as service of process docs and notices on your LLC's behalf from the State of Indiana.

https://inbiz.in.gov/start-business

Iowa

To register an LLC in Iowa, visit the Iowa Secretary of State Business Entity Forms and Fees webpage and help page on forming a Limited

Liability Company in the State of Iowa using the links provided below. The help page will walk you through filing a document to form an Iowa limited liability company selecting the LLC or professional LLC chapter for your business, naming your business, and setting an expiration date for your registry or electing to register a Perpetual LLC. https://help.sos.iowa.gov/how-do-i-form-llc https://sos.iowa.gov/business/formsandfees.html

Kansas

To register an LLC in Kansas, visit the State of Kansas Office of the Secretary of State Business Center using the link provided below. This web page will guide you through setting up an account to use Kan Access to file forms with the Kansas Department of State online and access your records from the Office of the Secretary of State.

The Business Center has everything you need to file a Kansas domestic or foreign LLC or LP (limited partnership), order a Certificate of Good Standing, check name availability for your business and reserve a name, and file a change of resident agent.

https://www.kansas.gov/businesscenter/

Kentucky

To register an LLC in Kentucky, visit the Commonwealth of Kentucky Business OneStop page using the link provided below.

The page will guide you through the process of choosing your business' name and LLC structure, register your LLC with the state, get your state tax numbers, ensure you meet insurance requirements, get any necessary licenses and permits your business needs in the Commonwealth of Kentucky, and apprise you of all your state regulatory compliance and employer responsibilities in Kentucky.

https://onestop.ky.gov/start/Pages/default.aspx

Louisiana

To register an LLC in Louisiana, visit the Louisiana Secretary of State Business Services pages with a guide to starting a business in Louisiana and file business documents with the Louisiana Office of the Secretary of State using the links provided below.

The Business Services page on filing documents to register your LLC in Louisiana will guide you through filing to register online, direct you to the State of Louisiana geauxBIZ portal, check name availability, form a professional LLC if applicable to your business, and outline all document compliance requirements to do business in Louisiana.

https://www.sos.la.gov/BusinessServices/StartABusiness/Pages/default.aspx

https://www.sos.la.gov/BusinessServices/FileBusinessDocuments/Pages/default.aspx

Maine

To register an LLC in Maine, visit the Maine Department of the Secretary of State Bureau of Corporations, Elections, & Commissions corporations page on forming a limited liability company in the State of Maine, and Maine.gov business portal page for starting a business.

There you can find the State of Maine Business Answers Program provided by the Department of Economic & Community Development and the Maine Business Works Program, by the Maine Small Business Development Centers and Department of Economic and Community Development by using the links provided below.

https://www.maine.gov/sos/cec/corp/llc.html
https://www.maine.gov/portal/business/starting.html

Maryland

To register an LLC in Maryland, visit the State of Maryland Business Express page provided at the link below. The page has a menu of links for business owners looking to file documents to conduct business in the State of Maryland, including Business Documents & Certificates of Status, Registry documents for a new business, trade name, or tax account, and file forms for annual reports, property tax returns, and late penalty payments due in the State of Maryland.

https://egov.maryland.gov/businessexpress

Massachusetts

To form an LLC in Massachusetts, visit the Commonwealth of Massachusetts guide to Starting a New Business and web page on forming a limited liability company using the link provided below. The Starting a New Business page will guide you through the process of writing a business plan, getting training, counseling, and advice on business financing, state services and grants for businesses in Massachusetts, how to file a "Doing Business As" (DBA) Certificate, and getting a state tax ID and learning the tax rules.

The Commonwealth of Massachusetts page on forming a limited liability company provides links to all the state's laws and regulations pertaining to your LLC, court rules, file forms to register your LLC, and additional resources for LLCs in the state.

https://www.mass.gov/guides/starting-a-new-businesshttps://www.mass.gov/info-details/massachusetts-law-about-limited-liability-companies-and-limited-liability-partnerships

Michigan

To form an LLC in Michigan, visit the State of Michigan Corporations, Securities, and Commercial Licensing Corporations Division's web page on forming a limited liability company using the link provided below.

The page provides links to Michigan's Limited Liability Company Act of 1993, limited liability company file forms to register your business with the state, a list of filing requirements, how to name your LLC in Michigan, and how to list a resident agent with your registration.

https://www.michigan.gov/lara/bureau-list/cscl/corps/limited-liability-co

Minnesota

To form an LLC in Minnesota, visit the State of Minnesota Employment and Economic Development page on forming a limited liability company and the Minnesota Business Forms and Fees page on the Minnesota Office of the Secretary of State's Business & Liens website. using the links provided below.

The page provides guidance on filing Articles of Organization with the Secretary of State and paying the LLC filing fee, choosing a name for your Minnesota LLC, and getting a registered office and registered agent in the state.

https://mn.gov/deed/business/starting-business/organizing/forming-limited-liability.jsp

https://mn.gov/deed/business/starting-business/organizing/limited-liability.jsp

Mississippi

To form an LLC in Mississippi, visit the Mississippi Secretary of State

Business Services portal using the link provided below. You will have to register to create an account to log into the portal and access the state's resources to file your registration, pay your LLC filing fees, and get a commercial registered agent in the state.

https://corp.sos.ms.gov/corp/portal/c/portal.aspx

Missouri

To form an LLC in Missouri, visit the Missouri Secretary of State web page on Starting a Business and Office of the Secretary of State's Missouri small business guide using the links provided below.

The Starting a Business Page includes downloadable forms, online entity registration, information on Missouri business entities, entity name availability and requirements in the State of Missouri, and some business links to helpful organizations and government agencies.

The small business startup guide includes business entity benefits in the State of Missouri; basic steps in creating a business; pages on LLCs, LPs (limited partnerships), LLPs (limited liability partnerships), and Limited Liability Limited Partnership (LLLP); and a guide to foreign entity registration.

https://www.sos.mo.gov/business/corporations/startbusinesshttps:/
/www.sos.mo.gov/business/outreach/startup_guide

Montana

To form an LLC in Montana, visit the Office of the Secretary of State of Montana's "How do I…" page for business services and SOS Enterprise Online Business Services Filing Portal using the links provided below.

The "How do I..." page provides links to State of Montana resources to get a filing portal login, file annual reports for your Montana LLC, request business documents and certificates, register your LLC with the State of Montana, find a registered agent in the state, and register a trademark with the State of Montana.

https://sosmt.gov/business/how-do-i/

https://biz.sosmt.gov/

Nebraska

To form an LLC in Nebraska, visit the Nebraska Secretary of State web pages on New Business Information and Forms and Fee Information using the links provided below. The page on New Business Information provides resources on forming and naming your LLC, finding a registered agent in the state, and complying with State of Nebraska filing and corporate reporting rules.

The Forms and Fee Information page provides links to all the official State of Nebraska file forms for domestic and foreign limited liability companies, Nebraska series LLCs, Nebraska protected foreign series LLCs, and every form of limited liability general partnership available in Nebraska.

https://sos.nebraska.gov/business-services/new-business-information

https://sos.nebraska.gov/business-services/forms-and-fee-information

Nevada

To form an LLC in Nevada, visit the Nevada Secretary of State page to "Start a Business" and register a Limited Liability Company in the State of Nevada using the link provided below.

The page has all the links you need to form a Nevada LLC, a foreign Nevada LLC, a Nevada Professional LLC, processing dates in the State of Nevada, and other Nevada business entity resources.

https://www.nvsos.gov/sos/businesses/start-a-business/limited-liability-company

New Hampshire

To form an LLC in the state of New Hampshire, visit the New Hampshire Department of State Corporations web page on forming a domestic or foreign limited liability company using the link provided below. The page provides official state domestic and foreign LLC file forms. The State of New Hampshire LLC file fee schedule, and instructions to file to register your LLC in the State of New Hampshire by filing online or using a paper filing by postal mail.

https://sos.nh.gov/corporation-ucc-securities/corporation/forms-and-fees/domestic-and-foreign-limited-liability-company/domestic-forms/

New Jersey

To form an LLC in the State of New Jersey, visit the State of New Jersey Department of the Treasury Division of Revenue and Enterprise Services Online Business Formation Page, Getting Registered Page, and the Business.NJ.gov Register Your Business Page using the links provided below.

These three official State of New Jersey pages will provide you with all the information and resources you need in the state of New Jersey for Starting a Business, filing Requirements, and Additional Resources for business in the state of New Jersey.

The Register Your Business Page also includes Industry Starter Kits, Business Names services, forms to register your business, tax registration forms, out of state business and registration, and requirements for hiring and managing employees in the State of New Jersey.

https://www.njportal.com/dor/businessformation/home/welcome

https://www.state.nj.us/treasury/revenue/gettingregistered.shtml

https://business.nj.gov/pages/register-your-business?locale=en

New Mexico

To form an LLC in New Mexico, visit the New Mexico Office of the Secretary of State Start a business web page on the official website's Business Services site. The page provides all the resources you need to e-file or paper file a Domestic or Foreign New Mexical LLC registration with the State of New Mexico.

https://www.sos.nm.gov/business-services/start-a-business/domestic-nm-llc/

New York

To form an LLC in New York, visit the New York State Department of State web page on Forming a Limited Liability Company in New York using the link provided below. The page includes a frequently asked Questions and Answers section, how to choose a name for your LLC in New York State, and instructions for completing Articles of Organization. https://dos.ny.gov/forming-limited-liability-company-new-york

North Carolina

To form an LLC in the state of North Carolina, visit the North Carolina Secretary of State website for Preparing the Documents and Attachments to Register Your Business in the state of North Carolina using the link provided below.

The page provides links to North Carolina requirements for starting LLCs, Limited Partnerships, Limited Liability Partnerships, Limited Liability Limited Partnerships, and Professional LLC as well as other links to North Carolina state resources for businesses in North Carolina.

https://www.sosnc.gov/Guides/launching_a_business/preparing_the_document_and_attachments

North Dakota

To form an LLC in the state of North Dakota, visit the business section of the office of the Secretary of State of North Dakota's official Portal for North Dakota State Government using the link provided below. The page provides a link to State of South Dakota Business Records Search, LLC and Professional LLC formation, Business Entity Statistics, Trade Name and Trademark Services registry, Copyright and Patent resources, and a link to State of South Dakota limited liability company statutes.

https://sos.nd.gov/business/business-services/business-structures/limited-liability-companies/limited-liability-company-llc.html

Ohio

To form an LLC in Ohio, visit the Ohio Secretary of State Business Services page with LLC Articles of Organization Filing Forms and Fee

Schedule for Domestic (Ohio) Business Entities and Foreign (Non-Ohio) Business Entities, as well as the Office of the Secretary of State of Ohio's QuickStart guide to starting a limited liability in Ohio using the links provided below.

https://www.ohiosos.gov/businesses/filing-forms--fee-schedule/

https://www.ohiosos.gov/globalassets/publications/busserv/llc.pdf

Oklahoma

To form an LLC in Oklahoma, visit the State of Oklahoma Department of Commerce Quick Reference Guide Page to starting a business in Oklahoma and the State of Oklahoma official Articles of Organization filing form for new limited liability companies in Oklahoma, using the links provided below.

https://www.okcommerce.gov/doing-business/startups-entrepreneurs/how-to-start-a-business/

https://www.sos.ok.gov/forms/fm0074.pdf

Oregon

To form an LLC in Oregon, visit the State of Oregon Office of the Secretary of State web page Business Section using the link provided below. The left sidebar navigation menu on the page has links to the Oregon Secretary of State's guides and official file forms to register, renew, or reinstate a business in the State of Oregon.

The secretary of state's office business section also has a frequently requested services page for businesses organized in the State of Oregon, a Find a Business engine, Business Information Center, the State of Oregon Uniform Commercial Code, Business Records and Statistics, a

License Directory, and state resources for Small Business Assistance.

https://sos.oregon.gov/business/pages/domestic-limited-liability-companies-forms.aspx

https://sos.oregon.gov/business/Pages/business-registration-forms.aspx

Pennsylvania

To form an LLC in Pennsylvania, visit the Commonwealth of Pennsylvania's Department of State website Business Resources section on forming a limited liability company in the State of Pennsylvania and the Department of State registration file forms page using the links provided below.

https://www.dos.pa.gov/BusinessCharities/Business/Resources/Pages/Pennsylvania-Limited-Liability-Company.aspx

https://www.dos.pa.gov/BusinessCharities/Business/RegistrationForms/Pages/default.aspx

Rhode Island

To form an LLC in Rhode Island, visit the Rhode Island Department of State web page on starting a Rhode Island Business using the link provided below. It will guide you through the state's process to register a unique business name in the state of Rhode Island, find a registered agent to include with your filing, provide the state with proof of insurance and board approval, register your business, confirm your filing, and register with the Rhode Island Division of Taxation, as well as get a Federal Employer Identification Number (EIN).

https://www.sos.ri.gov/divisions/business-services/ri-business/start-your-rhode-island-business

South Carolina

To form an LLC in South Carolina, visit the South Carolina Secretary of State office's Online Filings page, Business Entities Index page to File, Search, and Retrieve documents electronically, Business Resources page, and Downloadable Paper Forms page using the links provided below.

https://sos.sc.gov/online-filings

https://businessfilings.sc.gov/businessfiling

https://sos.sc.gov/business-resouces

https://businessfilings.sc.gov/BusinessFiling/Home/DownloadForm s

South Dakota

To form an LLC in South Dakota, visit the South Dakota Secretary of State Division of Business Services page on forming a limited liability in the State of South Dakota using the links provided below. The Division of Business Services page has resources to Register a Business in South Dakota, Search for Business Information, File an Annual Report, get a South Dakota sales tax license, check business name availability, find a commercial registered agent to include with your filing, trademark registration, get a federal employer identification number (EIN), and get a Certificates of Good Standing/Existence from the State of South Dakota.

https://sdsos.gov/business-services/corporations/corporate-forms/limited-liability-companies.aspx

Tennessee

To form an LLC in Tennessee, visit the Tennessee Secretary of State web center on Businesses, Business Entity Registration, and Business Forms and Fees using the links provided below. The official State of Tennessee Businesses page includes resources for in-state and out-of-state filers to file annual reports for your LLC, register a new business online, search businesses, file and search uniform commercial codes, and order copies and certificates.

https://sos.tn.gov/businesses

https://tnbear.tn.gov/newbiz/

https://sos.tn.gov/businesses/forms-and-fees

Texas

To form an LLC in Texas, visit the Texas Secretary of State Business Services web page on with links to online searches and filings, where to upload documents online, tracking and other searches, general information for new and existing businesses and starting a new business in the State of Texas, business FAQs, business forms, the Texas Uniform Commercial Code, and State of Texas Fees, Legal, and other information using the link provided below.

https://www.sos.state.tx.us/corp/index.shtml

Utah

To form an LLC in Utah, visit the Utah Department of Commerce Division on Corporations and Commercial Code Online Business Registration page, State of Ohio Considerations on Forming a Limited Liability Company page, and Domestic Limited Liability Company page using the links provided below.

https://corporations.utah.gov/business-entities/domestic-limited-liability-company/

https://corporations.utah.gov/business-entities/considerations-in-forming-a-limited-liability-company/

https://corporations.utah.gov/online-business-registration/

Vermont

To form an LLC in Vermont, visit the Vermont Secretary of State Business Services Division website, the Register a Business in Vermont page, the Vermont Secretary of State web page on forming a limited liability company, and the Domestic Business Registration web page for business in Vermont using the links provided below.

https://sos.vermont.gov/corporations/

https://sos.vermont.gov/corporations/registration/domestic-registration/llc/

https://sos.vermont.gov/corporations/registration/

https://sos.vermont.gov/corporations/registration/domestic-registration/

Virginia

To form an LLC in the Commonwealth of Virginia, visit the Commonwealth of Virginia's State Corporation Commission (SCC) Clerk's Information System (CIS) , the Commonwealth of Virginia's Start a New Business page, and the Virginia State Corporation Commission's page on forming a limited liability company in Virginia using the links provided below.

https://cis.scc.virginia.gov/

https://www.scc.virginia.gov/pages/New-Business-Resources

https://scc.virginia.gov/pages/Virginia-Limited-Liability-Companies

Washington

To form an LLC in Washington State, visit the State of Washington's Office of the Secretary of State web page on forming a limited liability company with online and paper registrations to form a Washington LLC or foreign (non-Washington LLC) and the Secretary of State Office's Download Forms page for Business entities using the links provided below.

https://www.sos.wa.gov/corporations-charities/business-entities/limited-liability-companies-llc-online-and-paper-registrations

https://www.sos.wa.gov/corporations-charities/business-entities/download-forms

West Virginia

To form an LLC in West Virginia, visit the West Virginia State Agency Directory for Online Services West Virginia One Stop Business Portal at Business4 WV to find the State of West Virginia's quick links menu to the Office of the Secretary of State's Business Startup Wizard, Business Fundamentals Workshop, Start a West Virginia Business guide, access the West Virginia MyTaxes portal, and find other resources for LLCs in the state, using the link provided below.

https://business4.wv.gov/Pages/default.aspx

Wisconsin

To form an LLC in Wisconsin, visit the State of Wisconsin Department of Revenue New Business home page and Open My Business at Wisconsin One Stop using the links provided below.

https://www.revenue.wi.gov/Pages/Businesses/New-Business-home.aspx

https://onestop.wi.gov/OpenMyBusiness

Wyoming

To form an LLC in Wyoming, visit the Wyoming Office of the Secretary of State's home page on Business and Uniform Commercial Code to Start a Business, file online to make annual reports to the State of Wyoming, find a commercial registered agent, obtain a certificate of good standing online, and access State of Wyoming online business services using the link provided below.

https://sos.wyo.gov/business/startabusiness.aspx

Book #2

How To Write a Business Plan and What to Consider When Starting a Business

Who's Your Business Plan For?

"You've got to eat while you dream. You've got to deliver on short-range commitments, while you develop a long-range strategy and vision and implement it. The success of doing both if you will. Getting it done in the short-range, and delivering a long-range plan, and executing on that."
Jack Welch

So, you're ready to write a business plan. Congratulations!

Most of the economy's workers are operators, managers, or developers. They operate, manage, or develop some aspect of a business that already exists.

That's a great way for most workers to make a living, a high-income wage or salary, or even to become wealthy over a successful career, with smart household budgeting and consistent investing in growth and value assets, using tax-advantaged long-term savings accounts.

But if you've decided to start a business, then you want to take on the mental work, the risk, and the extra time and effort to find new opportunities to create value for your customers that are under-utilized, or completely unnoticed or ignored by the rest of the industry's participants.

Most new businesses starting from scratch are led by founders who operate, manage, and develop the business themselves to understand it, refine it, and perform the work themselves that it requires to get customers, fulfill orders, and meet its administrative requirements.

They grow their businesses by delegating operations as they master them to employees, contract workers, and/or automated software apps. Writing your business plan will help you get a realistic overview of how your business works to deliver goods and yield profits.

If you take it seriously and put in the commensurate time and effort, writing your business plan could make the difference between a meager result from a tedious daily grind and making a small or large fortune from your business.

The most successful businesses in the world make fortunes for their owners that will last for lifetimes, and the most likely path to real income growth and true wealth creation is starting a business and leading it to success.

"No moral intuition is more hard-wired into Americans' concept of economic justice than equality of opportunity. The reason Americans tolerate higher levels of income inequality is because of our faith that we all have a fair chance at achieving the American Dream or becoming the next Bill Gates."
George Mason University professor, Dr. Steven Pearlstein (The Washington Post, 2018)

A Chicago Booth study found that over recent decades the number of billionaires on the Forbes 400 list were self-made entrepreneurs who started a business. Market research data reported by CNBC found that the world's ultra-wealthy, those with a net worth of $30 million or more, are mostly self-made millionaires who started their own business. In fact, 67.7% of them are.

Forbes did a study of its Forbes 400 list in 2019 and found that almost half of the entrepreneurs on the list started a business before the age of 30. The average age each started their first business was 32. Most of them (85%) had started a business by the age of 40. Another 15% of the founders on the list launched their first venture in their 40s or 50s.

Who Your Business Plan Is for Will Guide How You Write It

As you write your business plan, keep in mind your purpose for writing it and the intended audience or recipient of your completed plan.

Who are you writing it for, what key information will you need to communicate, and how do you communicate that effectively in your business plan?

1. **Is the business plan an exercise** for you and other key principals of your business:

    a. To test and refine your business as a simulation

    b. Using as much real-world data as you can get

    c. To learn your business as much as possible

    d. Before committing the time, effort, and money to it you'll learn what it requires from making the plan.

    e. And meanwhile producing a document that:

        ■ Guides your leadership and management of the business

        ■ Outlines how it produces cash flows and profits

        ■ Summarizes all the relevant factors in your business?

2. **Is it to get a business loan** from a bank, private lender, or someone you know, to get going with the cash you are estimating your company will require up front in fixed costs to get established and begin transacting business?

Whether that's for:

    a. Tools and equipment

b. Supplies and inventory

c. An advertising budgets

d. Incorporation expenses, attorneys' fees, licensing, and insurance

e. Or other fixed costs, or some combination of these?

3. **Is it to get VC funds** from a venture capitalist to scale quickly?

Because you:

a. Have a reliable profit model from the promotion and advertising of a product, service, brand, app, or some other kind of business,

b. You are thinking you and the business are ready to go on a customer, user, or subscriber acquisition spree that will rapidly scale your business,

c. In exchange for a percentage of your business's equity and creative control?

Every effective business plan is for the founder first and foremost, but you may also be writing your plan for the reasons in items 2 or 3 above.

This book will outline business plan writing as an exercise for founders in detail, but it will also cover the basics of writing a business plan to get a business loan and venture capital equity financing. The first chapter, "Understanding Market Research," will cover:

- The Purpose of Market Research

- Market Research Tactics for the 2020s

- Learning The Market Scientifically

- Case Studies / Examples of Market Research

CHAPTER 1

Understanding Market Research

The purpose of a business is to serve the market and its success or failure is decided by the market. So, market research in the planning of a business can on no account be neglected.

Business theorists have long debated whether the purpose of business is to serve the owners of the business by increasing their profits, or to serve society by providing a profitable living for workers, while maintaining a social consciousness and investing profits back into the community.

Either way, the nature and conditions of the market and the array of decisions made by its participants are the beginning and end of a business. Profits are the market's mechanism for rewarding and thus incentivizing businesses to solve a problem for them.

The market's participants are at liberty to choose how they spend their money, and have an enormous— and constantly growing and changing— variety of choices in businesses to pay, finance, or capitalize on in exchange for having an endless number of problems solved that people like to pay to have solved. Your business plan is to be part of that growth and change.

Learning The Market Scientifically

Although the entire market doesn't exist in a laboratory, some of the variables within it that are of key importance to your business can certainly be studied scientifically. The business planner who is adept at studying the market scientifically to find business opportunities and develop them may soon find themselves managing the market scientifically.

Using the always growing and improving variety of tools available for conducting commerce over the Internet, entrepreneurs can quickly and affordably access current market data:

- To find out who our customers are

- To find out what problems we can solve for them

- To find out what solutions they like for other problems they have

- To find out what they're reading, listening to, or watching, and what application ecosystems and environments they're using, so we can advertise to them

The customer you might find is ideal for your business through your marketing research, may not even know they have the problem your product or service solves, until your advertising brings it to their attention and your product or service solves it for them.

Hence the market value of social media platforms like Gmail, YouTube, TikTok, Reddit, LinkedIn, Instagram, Pinterest, Snapchat, Facebook, and Twitter.

On the other hand, the customer you might find is most ideal for your business as you conduct your market research, may know exactly what their problem is and are looking for the solution, motivated buyers credit card ready in hand to pay to get it fixed for them.

Hence the market value of search engines like Google, Bing, Yahoo, and Baidu.

These motivated customers looking for a known solution to a problem they have may find a better solution you have for them if they find you when they go to look.

Finding and paying for a known solution saves them time and headache learning something to solve the problem themselves that someone else has already learned and can solve immediately.

It saves them time and mental resources to concentrate on the problems they specialize in solving so they can become more productive and serve their clients better whether they have a book of business or work at a job for a company with a department or division as their primary customer.

If they're looking for another specialist in the economy to solve their problem for them with money in hand to pay to have it solved, then most likely they have the extra funds to pay to get their problem solved and not the extra time to learn how and fix it themselves because they have a successful business, whether it's a career at a company they work for or a business they started.

There is a lot of money out there. It's in fact an ocean of money out there brimming, over every year with more. You can dive into that ocean and drink as much as you want and not even make a dent in it. Go out and get yours and start paying to have your problems solved by specialists too instead of solving them yourself. The economy is rich with solutions found by specialists.

Ad Campaigns, A/B Testing, Cost Per Thousands Impression

These are the basics of Internet market research and advertising whether you're using social media platforms or search engines as your primary way of reaching your customers:

- Cost Per Thousand impressions (CPM– yes, that's a Latin letter there)

- Click Thru Rate of impressions (CTR)

- Conversion Rate Optimization of CTR (CRO)

- Unit Sales Price, Cost of Fulfillment, and Profit

- Running Ad and Sales Creative

Your cost per thousand impressions or CPM is your dollar ad spend to get your advertisement to show up on the page for a thousand visitors. The percentage of them that clicks your ad taking them to the page with your message and offer is your click thru rate or CTR.

The percentage of those visitors that engage with your message and offer and make the decision to place an order today is your conversion rate. CRO or conversion rate optimization is the methodical and data-based process of A/B testing refinements to the ad placement, audience, and creative, the sales message, or the product or offer to increase the conversion rate.

Your unit sales price or average order sales price minus your cost of fulfillment is your profit per order. That figure times the number of orders you take, receive payment for, and fulfill in a period like a month, quarter, or year, is the total profit from the operation of your business. Ostensibly, you want to have a total profit that is worth the business plan to you.

Ad and sales creative is the design of the prospect's journey from where they were when they saw your advertisement, to your message and offer page, and ideally the decision to purchase your product or service.

It includes the copy, visual, or audio for the advertisement and the wider context of the platform they run on and the content they run against, as well as the timing and zeitgeist of the market.

Case Studies/Examples of Successful Market Research

The following pair of case studies serve as examples of successful market research that might help you to generate some ideas and strategies of your own to conduct market research and organize your business plan. The case studies briefly summarize:

- Jeff Bezo's approach to understanding the market in terms of industries that followed historical parallels to the Internet, in order to grow Amazon to dominate e-commerce.

- Peter Thiel's approach to scaling PayPal to its widest possible addressable market for making instant, low-fee e-cash payments from your phone or desktop computer

PayPal - Marketing A Simple Solution to A Focused Segment to Achieve Scale

When Peter Thiel and Elon Musk launched PayPal as a merger of Confinity and X.com, they were looking to scale it to be a serious competitor to the U.S. dollar itself for active users and volumes. That's what Peter Thiel has said in retrospect of the world historical scale of their ambitions for the business they were planning to build.

But they didn't start off trying to get everyone to use their instant, low-fee, and convenient electronic cash service. What they did was very intentionally target a smaller, defined market where there was a hook that would make their product understandable and welcome there to quickly reach scale within that network.

This would generate the initial proof of the product's value and revenues to pay for bringing the product to market, giving the company more bargaining power over its equity when it would be time to scale with capital, while making it a more attractive opportunity for capitalists to invest in.

PayPal began studying the market's possibilities for the penetration of its product by advertising it to Blackberry users. They found that this test market wasn't successful for PayPal. The only thing they had in common was they used Blackberry phones, and that didn't have enough of a connection to a problem that PayPal could solve.

So, PayPal did some more market research to find a suitable market that would readily sign up in large percentages to use PayPal's service. They decided on marketing directly to eBay users with merchant seller accounts to use PayPal's service to accept payments online made with credit and debit cards.

That worked to get PayPal's business going. After finding a segment of online participants that would most directly benefit from their product in a way that would be obvious to them as soon as it was advertised to them, PayPal had a steady, growing stream of customers and orders.

PayPal soon became the default and most commonly used payment method on eBay. From there it was able to get a sales team and grow its business rapidly using the revenues from its customers and rounds of financing and investment. By 2002, PayPal was acquired by eBay for $1.5 billion shortly after its IPO.

Amazon - Understanding Market Trends in Terms of Historical Developments

When Jeff Bezos started Amazon, he didn't just make a business plan in terms of how some numbers relate to some spreadsheets, even though that's an important part of it.

He planned his business and conducted his research of the market with a sense of historical context and parallels.

This is useful because history repeats itself in business, commerce, and industry, and the birth and development of new industries follow a number of comparable trends.

Contextualizing market research in terms of trends that have historical parallels helps entrepreneurs to anticipate the direction of the markets their businesses trade in.

As a result, startups can be more effective at designing a product and offer that intersects with the market in a way that results in a trend of sustainable growth for the business.

In an illuminating 2003 presentation entitled, "The electricity metaphor," Amazon founder Jeff Bezos says that the tempting analogy for the 1990s Internet boom and subsequent early 2000s NASDAQ bust— is the 1840s Gold Rush to California.

But Bezos argues that the more technically true analogy to the Internet is the first industry for mass market electricity and electrical appliances, "If we look at what happened in the Internet, it was such an incredible last half a dozen years that it's hard to get the right analogy for it."

"The part of the electric revolution," that made it like the Internet is how it ushered in, "a golden age of appliances," Bezos contends.

"The killer app that got the world ready for appliances is the lightbulb. The lightbulb is what wired the world and they weren't thinking about appliances when they wired the world. They weren't putting electricity into the home. They were putting lighting into the home."

It would be impossible for the author to guess what historical developments bear useful parallels to the trends happening in the relevant industries and markets for your business plan, however, you may have a hunch or idea based on what topics genuinely interest you that you spend your free or leisure time enjoying learning about.

Even if a hobby, interest, or passion of yours may seem unrelated to your business or business plan, they both have at least you and your mind in common. It may be that you found an interest in it because of pre-knowledge or intuition that there is something of value there to be found that you can use to think about your business.

Here are some leads to follow to do your own regular general historical research about business as part of your self-directed, continuing education to help support your business acumen with a wider and more detailed base of general business history knowledge:

- The NASDAQ / Dot Com Boom and Bust in 2000

- The Housing Market Boom and 2008 Financial Crisis

- The 2010s Birth of Cryptocurrency and Blockchain

- Joint Stock Organization From 1600s to Wall Street

- English Common Law and the Printing Press Revolution

- Adam Smith, Industrial Revolution, Standard Parts and Assembly Lines

- The Electric Industry from General Electric to Tesla

- The Petroleum Industry and the Automobile Revolution

- The Television Industry, Mass Marketing, and Professional Advertising

- The Music Industry, R&D, and Patent and Copyright History

Jeff Bezos followed the lessons from the historical development of the electrical appliance industry to spot the enormous opportunity promised by the fast-accelerating growth of Internet subscriptions in the 1990s.

At the time, Bezos, who was raised by poor immigrants to the United States, had a very lucrative salary and key role as a senior vice president applying mathematical modeling to optimize and build financial security systems for a high-grossing hedge fund in New York City.

It was a job most people consider something like a career pinnacle, but Bezos quit his well-paying, secure and stable job with an established and reputable company to strike out on his own and start a bookstore made possible by the Internet— one with the widest selection in history, that you could peruse from home on your computer, and place an order to be shipped right to your door.

Like PayPal did later, Amazon scaled by targeting a small enough segment that its business would be able to concentrate its resources to achieve a sustainable business in the first place.

Then Amazon moved into adjacent market segments to develop and expand the business, ones with similarities to the market where Amazon had proved and achieved mastery over its core competencies and their implementation to serve a customer base.

Learning more about the applicable lessons from the early successes of these businesses could greatly enrich your thinking as you develop your business plan.

CHAPTER 2

Analyzing the Market

Analyzing the market for your business plan means breaking down what you're thinking and what you're learning about the market into their smallest meaningful pieces and assembling them into a model of the market and your business as a machine within it.

That model is your business plan, but the real magic of creation happens when you begin to move those models onto other media that continue to model your business in fine enough detail to apply to the market. Then your model becomes a working model. Then your working model becomes a business.

As you run messages to the market that communicate your business plan to prospective customers as an enticement and offer, and keep records of your business's communications, engagements, and transactions, you are testing how your plan interacts with the market for real and developing a database of records to find what doesn't work to cut from your budget and efforts, and what does work to double down on and to generate more ideas to test.

Growing your business from a plan into an operation that delivers real goods to the market for payment, can feel surprisingly and miraculously like writing a story so well that with your guidance, initiative, and motivation, it climbs out of the page and into the world and becomes a real incorporation of the market economy.

Identifying Your Business's Target Market

Michael Dell, the founder of Dell Computers, sold enough newspaper subscriptions in high school to make more money than his teacher for the year.

By the time he started college at the University of Texas, he drove a white BMW with his computers and electronics in tow.

Dell sold so many newspaper subscriptions by identifying his business' target market. He might have simply tried the brute force method of the door-to-door salesman.

That's a method of data collection called canvassing, the shotgun approach, spray and pray, or throw the pasta at the wall and see what sticks.

Experience and statistical science both tell you that he would have wasted most of his time talking to prospects who already had newspaper subscriptions or didn't have one because they weren't in the market for one.

Instead, Dell did some thinking about his results after doing some canvassing and realized his only buyers were newlyweds or people who had just bought a home and recently moved in.

These were typically young or middle-aged people having some success in life and taking optimistic steps forward with big long-term commitments.

Like the address and mailbox were like the lightbulb of Jeff Bezos' analogy for the Internet. In fact, it wasn't really much different from the Internet in the basics, just slower to operate and send messages, with the use of heavier media.

Getting new addresses, and putting different names on your postage, in the 1970s was like setting up your new smartphone, computer, email address, and social media handles.

The enthusiasm and fun of setting up this application ready, general conduit for communications to the new household or newlywed couple was fresh on their minds.

Naturally when offered a newspaper subscription, they had the motivated desire to subscribe to papers other than from their friends written by professional organizations to the public with a variety of columns covering news topics of the day, politics, business, markets, the arts, and the Sunday comics.

So, an enterprising Dell got ahold of the county court records of new marriages and listings of housing sales that recently closed, and addressed all his efforts to sell newspapers to these prospects. That's a great example of how to find your target market.

Understanding Market Trends

Bestselling business book author Seth Godin's business philosophy is simple with endless applications. Find a world and a way to be the best in the world at something. This isn't easy and takes time, but the rewards for the effort are greatly disproportionate when you become the best in the world, the linchpin of an industry, a company, a company division, or a market.

As it turns out, with the level of granularity and modularity our Internet-connected tooling allows us today, it seems possible for an endless number of new businesses to emerge that become the linchpin of solving some remarkably simple problems for a vast marketplace of customers, because they're the best in the world at it and the problem keeps coming up somewhere.

You become an expert at something to understand the relevant market trends impacting your business plan. Your vision doesn't have to be as limited as to get in a market and make out with x number of dollars every reporting period delivering goods to that market.

That can be a perfectly suitable way to make a living and go into business. It's what franchise owners do, setting up and operating readymade businesses with a working business plan, brand, and marketing already done for them.

Along the more DIY ethos of the Internet marketplace, you might also find a replicable profitable business model that works and that you like and run with it to start a business of your own.

But from there you might find your more detailed view of the marketplace turns up leads— opportunities to become an expert at solving a valuable problem to solve for your market.

Or you might set out in the first place to become an expert at solving some problem, by doing something your competitors or your customers do repeatedly, having as much familiarity with the process as they do, and more familiarity than they do with something else you bring to the process that helps you find a better way to do it, a way that saves money or time, or improves features and experiences for users or consumers of the application or product.

Conducting a SWOT Analysis

The SWOT analysis as an organizational management and planning tool for business has been an essential part of business strategy since the 1960s. Some form of it originated at the Lockheed Martin Corporate Development Planning Department in 1952.

By the 1960s it was promoted around the Stanford Research Institute by two business planning research consultants, Robert Franklin Stewart and Albert Humphrey as SOFT:

> "What is good in the present is Satisfactory, good in the future is
> an Opportunity; bad in the present is a Fault, and bad in the future
> is a Threat."

Across the continent four colleagues working at the Harvard Graduate School of Business Administration put together the basis for SWOT for a textbook that ran for many editions, entitled, "Business Policy: Text and Cases." The textbook summarized it thusly:

> "Deciding what strategy should be is, at least ideally, a rational undertaking. Its principal sub activities include identifying opportunities and threats in the company's environment and attaching some estimate of risk to the discernible alternatives. Before a choice can be made, the company's strengths and weaknesses must be appraised."

The current terminology for thinking of a business in the Ivy League at the time was Business Policy, though by the 21st-century business schools were more likely to formulate it as Business Strategy or Strategic Management.

That's a coinage with connotations of moving faster, with colder vibes, and steadier movement while maintaining a vigilant, current, and prescient external market and environmental awareness to guide policy and action— from the highest levels of international corporate competition among titans of industry to the small, agile, upstart networks of information workers and automated machinery entering the fray with the lowest barriers to entry in the history of industry.

Under Jack Welch's tenure as CEO of General Electric starting in 1981, the company enjoyed another golden era and massive return to profitability, growing revenues from $12 billion a year when he took over as CEO to $410 billion by the time he retired.

His policy was simple and can be applied to focus your business plan from the beginning as you do the market research for your business. He had one overarching vision and rule to guide General Electric's strategy under his leadership: It had to lead sales as #1 or #2 in a segment it participated in or be able to with some strategic thinking and action, or divest its commitments to keep production in those industries.

Two Jack Welch quotes that summarize strategic vision and thinking for businesses that excel at winning sales and customers are: "Good business leaders create a vision, articulate the vision, passionately own the vision and relentlessly drive it to completion." "Any jerk can have short-term earnings. You squeeze, squeeze, squeeze, and the company sink five years later."

Porter's Five Forces Competitor Analysis

The Five Forces framework for market competitor analysis as a microeconomic model of market forces. Originated by Michael E. Porter as a supplementary tool to SWOT to fill in some gaps in the less complete SWOT analysis, it was first published in the Harvard Business Review in 1979.

Three of the Five Forces are composed of "Horizontal Competition," 1.) Substitute Products and Services, 2.) Incumbent Rivals, 3.) and New Entrants. The other two of the Five Forces consist of "Vertical Competition," in the form of the Bargaining Power of 4.) Suppliers and 5.) Customers.

These vertical aspects of competition are essentially the determinants of supply and demand in industrial organization economics for factory assembly lines of production.

The horizontal aspects of competition are:

- What are all the solutions that your target customers are buying today to fix their problem, or buying instead of fixing their problem, that they might trade out for your solution and offer?

- Is your business plan trying to do something that has already been done by an incumbent that completely dominates the market for it in brand, reputation, and user statistics.

- What are the fixed costs of entering the market you are trying to serve, the expenses that must be paid in order to produce just the first unit of your product, before your per unit cost for each additional unit of production?

(Fixed costs in time, money, effort, information, awareness, capability, competency, reliability, consistency, characteristics, advantage, opportunity?)

The answers to these questions and ones like them you think of as you do your market research will help you to understand the economic distributions and forces in your relevant markets.

CHAPTER 3

Developing a Business Plan

You may likely develop your business plan as you conduct your research and market analysis. This chapter will cover the most common elements of a business plan with some ideas to help you along, as well as how to create your own business model canvas. Finally, this chapter will cover the basics of financial projections and forecasting for the various types of business plans.

Elements of a Business Plan

Executive Summary - Your executive summary could include a headline that immediately grabs the reader with a shockingly good promise that your business plan can deliver. The rest of it may give a glimpse into how the plan works with an enticement to read the plan, address and answer the questions you may be confident or relatively sure the reader will have after reading your value proposition, or summarize the key points covered by your business plan. Write it to show off the astonishing value of your business while maintaining a curiosity gap so that it's compelling for the reader to read your plan to learn how it works.

Company Intro - Your company intro could provide the reader— whomever your primary, secondary, and tertiary readers are if you have that many different levels of readers for your business plan— with an introduction that talks about your company while developing the ideas in your executive summary. You might anticipate some of the next questions readers of your business plan will have while reading the executive summary and address those questions in your company intro.

Market Analysis - Your market analysis section could present your market research with your SWOT analysis and your Five Forces analysis for your industry and market. That way your reader will get a high-level overview of your business, industry, and market from you. The more your work on your plan the more you want to make your market analysis as realistic as possible

Industry Analysis - Your industry analysis could include observations and conclusions about your competitors, your industry's customers, and the goods your industry creates or uses to create. You may, along the way of summarizing your expertise in your industry, offer some theories as to why your competitors haven't produced a product or service like yours.

Customer Analysis - Your customer analysis could include demographic information about your customers, but these are fairly broad categories. Your business plan might also include customer segmentation by varying buyer motivations, ways, and means. It might also include the most common search queries that connect buyers with your offer or the social media interests they have in common for your business's advertising campaigns.

Marketing Plan - The more engagements with the market you have to measure the results and compare with all your data, the more realistic your market analysis can be. In your marketing plan, you can tell the reader how your business creates the best product to solve the problem it is designed to solve, and cover the mechanics and finances of its advertising/sales models or history.

Key Operations and Processes - As if there were a different hat for each operation, you could just tell the reader all the different hats in your business's operations, real or planned. You could try to design the simplest flowchart you can of the key requirements, regular operations to conduct your business, and regular processes or subroutines within those operations.

Roadmap and Key Metrics - In the roadmap or calendar section of your business plan, you can lay out your projections and thoughts about the evolution of your business's key metrics over time. You may include targets, deadlines, and/or milestones that are important to your business.

Management Intro - Here you may introduce your team and any other key players in managing your business operations with any kind of accountability for meeting key sales metrics or administration and organization-keeping such as regulatory compliance officers or human resources department.

Financial Plan - Your financial plan may include your business' assets/liabilities statement and balance sheet, your cash flow statements or financial reports, and your financial projections over relevant future terms. You may have some idea of the value of your business based on a detailed enough history of its cash flows to expenses and its market opportunities.

Creating a Business Model Canvas

Since the mid-to-late 2000s, the Pigneur-Osterwalder Business Model Canvas, distributed under a Creative Commons license, has been a neat way to organize a business plan and visualize it with an all-in-one-view display. That way it can be reviewed daily or otherwise periodically and revised and updated as the plan or business or both develop.

The Business Model Canvas was developed into five parts by Pigneur prior to 2005. These were a business: 1.) Infrastructure, 2.) Offering, 3.) Customers, 4.) Finances, and 5.) Revenue Streams. By 2008 the model canvas had developed into nine "building blocks."

These are: 1.) Key Partners, 2.) Key Activities, 3.) Key Resources, 4.) Value Propositions, 5.) Customer Relationships, 6.) Channels, 7.)

Customer Segments, 8.) Cost Structure, 9.) Revenue Streams. These can be further subdivided with key headings under each block and all listed and outlined to give an all-in-one-place overview of the business.

Key partners can be more than just if you have a business partner or equity financier or professional advisor. It can also be apps that you use that you keep and generate some substantial portion of data on that are important to your business or that your operations currently rely on. Key activities can be listed, graphed, or info graphed out as a sales funnel or flow chart. Key resources can correspond with key activities as inputs and/or outputs.

Value propositions can be that attention-grabbing headline, short phrase pitch that makes a shockingly good promise that your business can deliver on or delivers on.

Customer relationships can outline why your customers like your product or service and why your business likes your customers and market. It can include testimonials or feedback from customers that supports your business's headline value proposition.

Channels can list out the ways your business sends messages to its prospects, clients, or partners. You might decide ahead of time when planning your business to create all new accounts with apps and social media platforms the business uses.

That makes it clean and easy to turn over the credentials for them to a buyer if you sell your business, or to different managers if your business grows and you get managers to handle different accounts.

Customer segments can outline the differences in how your customers find you, why they buy your product or service, or how they use your product or service.

You can list out any customer relations management software (CRM) or sales software you use to keep up with your customers.

Cost structure can show your fixed costs then marginal costs per sale for each customer or sales segment with shared fixed costs and similar marginal costs.

Revenue streams can be expressed in terms of marginal costs and rated fixed costs to show net profit from sales related to your business' value proposition.

Financial Projections and Forecasting

We talked earlier in Chapter 1 about your ad costs and costs to fulfill orders, as well as the per unit profits from the advertising operations your business uses to reach customers with your message and proposition.

But it can get more complicated than that over the long-term operation of your business. Here are some examples of other considerations you may include in your business plan to get a fuller accounting to help in appraising the financial value of your business.

- Expenses for customer acquisition, sales, and fulfillment

- Expenses for customer service, returns, and retention

- Expenses for general business administration, obligations, and liabilities

- Expenses for customer segmentation, repeat business, and upselling

- Expenses for business loans and financing, insurance, and fees

In addition to these expenses, you might include revenues from each of these line items:

- Revenues from customer acquisition, sales, and fulfillment

- Revenues from customer services, returns, and retention

- Revenues from organizational efficiency, tax literacy, and settlement

- Revenues from customer segmentation, repeat business, and upselling

- Revenues from financed activities, compliance, and utilities

The more of this you're not filling in with guesses, the more realistic your business plan is about how your business operates, because it is oriented toward data from your business's interactions with the market.

The more of it you are filling in with guesses, the more realism your business plan will require from an assembly of evidence and intelligently-founded assumptions about the way your business would interact with the market and the results if it followed your marketing/advertising / sales plan.

A business plan with a financial section rich in either or both: 1.) historical data/documentation from operations and 2.) future projections/evidence from research, can more likely serve to many advantages.

The more realistic and intelligent the plan is at delivering a profitable result that has a large room to scale, the more advantageous it will be for you and other stakeholders in the business.

It can serve to the advantage of the founder, to understand the long-term cash flow value of their business; and to the business loan officer or private equity investor; and to the prospective business partner; and also, to a prospective buyer for the business— or some part of the business you can readily sell or provide service for at a good rate of return.

CHAPTER 4

Crafting a Marketing Strategy

Your marketing strategy is the sum of your enticement, offer, and fulfillment and the relation they bear to the relevant confluence and confounding factors of the marketplace, as far as knowledge, experience, and data can prove.

You may craft your marketing strategy as you conduct your market research, develop your business plan and operate your business, and revise and optimize your marketing strategy that way.

This chapter has some overview level suggestions for marketing strategy, creating a marketing plan, identifying marketing channels, building brand identity and messaging, and measuring marketing success.

Definition of Marketing Strategy

While Don Draper of Sterling Cooper on Madison Avenue may not be real, here are some quotes that the professionals at AMC included in their award-winning television series about the New York marketing industry in the 1960s:

- "It's useless to be creative unless you can sell what you create."

- "You are the product. You feel something. That's what sells."

- "Make it simple, but significant."

- "Spend 50% of your time writing your headline."

There's no telling how much of his time it took Steve Jobs to write the advertising tagline "1,000 songs in your pocket" at Apple, but it's an effective enticement because it succinctly expresses what a leap forwards the iPod was for mobile music players.

Henry Ford started with the headline too, telling his engineers to make him a V-8 engine suitable for mass production, and firing any who told him it couldn't be done.

James Cameron's entire pitch for a sequel to the Aliens film that did okay in ticket sales, was just spelling ALIEN$ on a chalkboard with a dollar sign for the "s."

Writing and rewriting a good headline for your product as you develop your ideas and your business plan helps you to define a value proposition that isn't vague or unoriginal, one that more or less plainly describes a promise your product or service can deliver on.

Some successful businesses have an enormous amount of capability and use the headline to find a useful way to apply it to the market. Some successful businesses have a useful application for the market in mind and use the headline as a benchmark of the capability to achieve.

Creating a Marketing Plan

The marketing plan could be about how to create a compelling advertisement, offer, and result; time and position that product or service in the best possible advertising markets for your business plan, using any of the available apps, platforms, and tools for marketers that are well-suited for your plan; and fulfill on the customer experience and result to an excellent degree of satisfaction, perhaps using a customer relation management (CRM) or sales app.

The constraints of the marketing plan might include the financing for communications to advertise to prospective customers using social media or search engine campaigns, or other forms of digital advertising and marketing.

The microeconomics of the business's costs and revenues to produce and market a good or service could play out over enough engagements with the market, with enough liquidity in advertising budgets to refine and optimize for profits.

The marketing plan's constraints could also include an advertising strategy or campaign that does not get the attention of the market, an offer that does not result in sales or orders, a result that is unsatisfactory to some customers in the market it's tested in or to the entire market, or a value proposition and message that does not time and position well in a prevailing market sentiment, or place well on certain apps or in certain advertisement segments.

The strengths of the marketing plan could include a well-informed, realistic, and value-adding market strategy; an ample and sufficient budget to test ad campaigns within that strategy to find profitable markets and ad creatives to make ad placements; a customer base that influences its peers' purchasing decisions and a product or service that they want to tell their friends about; or good timing and market-aware, brand-conscious advertising that rides market headwinds or tailwinds.

Your marketing plan's opportunities could include a list of marketable product or service improvements; or they could be methods, techniques, tools, processes, or what have you for reducing the expenses of producing and/or marketing a product or service, to offer a better price or retain a bigger profit from sales; or they could be valuable solutions to problems that are possible for the business because of emerging new technologies and platforms.

Identifying Marketing Channels

You can identify marketing channels for your business by discerning what apps members of your target industry or customer base use and favor most, that make discretionary purchasing decisions based on advertising, and testing ads on those platforms and see how they perform.

Marketing channels you can test include:

- **Google**

  o Searches for your product or service

  o Searches for information about your industry or techniques

  o Searches for information about your locality

  o Same idea with Bing and Yahoo!

- **Facebook**

  o A/B test creatives and audience variables to get your ad campaigns to bring visitors to an offer that make a decision to do business with you

- **YouTube**

  o Go for short video ad creatives, or stick with banner advertisements in the app and on the website, on the world's largest video platform.

  o Get sponsored ads read by influencers with product links on video descriptions

  o Same idea with TikTok, Snap, Reddit, Twitter, and Pinterest

- **Instagram**

  o Advertise through the platform with ad manager

  o Advertise through accounts with influencer marketing

- Advertise through organic reach as an influencer

- Same idea with Discord, Telegram, and Twitch

- **Amazon**

  - Advertise your business's products with FBA shipping

  - Advertise your expertise with a KDP self-published book

  - Advertise through influencer marketing with KDP authors

  - Same idea with Walmart, eBay, Shopify, and Etsy

These are some leads for the reader to check out and to help you generate or reflect any good ideas for marketing channels you may know of yourself worth investigating to see if your marketing strategy and advertising can find plenty of customers there.

Building Brand Identity and Messaging

Because your marketing strategy is the sum of your enticement, offer, and fulfillment and the relation they bear to the marketplace, when planning your business, you can coordinate your messaging through these elements of your marketing strategy.

You may then hone your marketing messaging and brand identity for your product or company as you continue your market research, implement your business plan, and obtain sales for your business.

You might want to adapt your message for each platform or advertising vertical when building brand identity for your business or product and designing messaging and ad creatives.

For example, on search platforms an appropriate and success worthy format is "problem >> solution" messaging and "how to" organic content that ideally:

1.) Helps your prospective customer accomplish a DIY that you would be the one to ask about it especially if you have the best answer and promote it on search results

2.) Establishes your authority, expertise, and professionality; includes reputation, credibility, and success indicators; and makes the visitor trust your business.

3.) Subtly advertises you're a business, but doesn't immediately make a sales pitch and offer; and gets the prospect to like your brand to come back to later when they're looking to pay to have a problem solved and think you might be their guy for it

-OR-

Depending on the market, product, and sales, perhaps get your prospect— who found your perfect solution to a problem, expressed in a way that understands them— to fall in love with your brand enough to go looking for what you sell to buy some

-OR-

Takes the visitor from your ads and/or your organic result placements directly to your sales pitch and offer, featuring at least one realistic element that your prospect cares about that builds urgency for them to make the purchase before they leave the page

4.) Enrolls your new co-conspirator in your brand, so that the next time you have an offer that you know they will find very attractive, enticing, and a worthwhile bargain to place an order (send a deposit, sign up for a subscription, make a purchase, or whatever the business is), they will be happy to find out about it from your email announcement.

Meanwhile, to continue the example, on social media channels an appropriate and success worthy format is: "here's another one you'll like," based on the posts you see your customer base likes on each platform (they share it, they smash the like button, they leave the funniest comments on it), on a regular schedule with updates on certain days of the week.

Keeping the posts hitting on certain days of the week with current references or worthwhile interruptions, while organizing the content in themed posts with a weekly rotation, allows your audience to catch feelings for your brand because it's so on point, funny, and reliable with its social media posts.

Everyone's checking in and keeping time together over social media, on a party line, with all these different communities' cultures predominating in different corners of the platform, and an all-pervasive platform culture inherent to the context and medium of the platform.

So, if they're done well, you might find the audience enjoys posts like:

- How long has it been since something or until something (something important)

- Keeping anniversaries and important calendar dates (something relatable)

- Keeping watch together: Do you see what I see? (Something remarkable)

- Ideating and orienting: What's happening? What's this like? (Something funny)

These are just a handful of ideas.

There are any number of ways you can post to social media to grow and engage an audience that will enthusiastically buy or sign up at a high rate when they see an occasional advertisement, offer, invitation, event, or coupon posted for your business.

It's about putting something together in a combination that tailors the audience and offers to each other, and timing advertisements and sales promotions for when your market is apt to buy.

CHAPTER 5

Putting Your Plan into Action

You may build your business plan entirely before putting it into action with real-world market engagements, or design it in tandem with market tests of advertisements and offers.

Tim Ferriss' big contribution in the 4-Hour Work Week that made his book a bestseller was pushing readers to go ahead and put together an offer they can deliver on and ask for the sale.

Lining up a bunch of research from Google Surveys asking *if* they'll buy is not as good as asking them to buy because:

More will say yes to the survey question than take a real offer and make a purchase, and it's difficult to be certain— without getting the offer with its best foot forward to the markets that will value it most— what the difference will be between the survey's results and a real market test of an advertisement and offer, backed up by an organization ready to deliver and keep up with the customers.

A business plan with a steady, profitable series of real-world engagements over enough time as a proof of concept, a plan that already works, pays its expenses, and generates profits, is one that has more value and leverage to shop around and bargain if it wants to use financing or equity investing to scale, because it doesn't need them to scale, only to scale faster.

When putting your business plan into action, you will most likely want to finish and formalize your business plan, set goals, deadlines, and milestones for your business to reach for, establish a financial plan that balances your resources and marketing plan effectively, and find ways to track performance, revise goals, and adjust your strategy as you go.

The Business Plan

Your final business plan for review by founders and key principals— to share with lawyers, accountants, and financial advisors; an /or to share with partners, financers, and investors—

Can all be finished in one-word document or include a mix of word, spreadsheet, and slide presentation documents like a pitch deck, overhead slide presentation, or a large print-out of your business model canvas.

When sharing your business plan with third parties prospectively to partner with, finance, or invest in your business, you may want to be strategic about how much of the business's valuable workings and how much detail you want to reveal in the plan you present to them.

You may want to hold some of it back to reveal in the advanced stages of talks with potential partners as your organizations are driving toward the closure of a deal for a contract.

Establishing Goals and Milestones

It may not work for everybody, but Elon Musk is famous for setting lofty goals for production at the world-historical titans-of-industry league of doing business.

He's also famous for not hitting his impossibly demanding goals, yet stretching to achieve results that haven't been accomplished before because of those goals.

You might see if taking that enormous scale of ambition on for the scope of your business helps you to generate more powerful ideas or motivation to develop your business.

The power of goal-setting to spur teams on to achieve outsized success is part and parcel of human nature. It works in the sports arena. That's why Michael Jordan missed and made more shots than most other players.

It works in sales departments. That's why agents that contact the most leads and follow up with them the most get the most rejections and get the most sales.

Setting goals does not mean your business will achieve them, or if it does that your business will achieve them as soon as you think or by the means you expect at first.

What setting goals does mean is that your business has clearly defined accountability for the key factors in production, sales, customer service, professionality, and administration.

Individuals, households, and organizations as simple as a small business with a sole proprietor and as sophisticated as entire nations find that by setting goals, they are more likely to move toward them.

Goal setting anchors the motivation of your business's key principals to push the operations that find profitability and expand a profitable business.

Failing without enough goals can lead to confusion, shock, and dissipation of a business's motivation and resolve.

Failing against a goal can led to focus, thinking, and concentration of a business's motivation and resolve. Not having or focusing on goals can lead to failure which leads to nowhere.

Setting and tracking performance against some good goals can lead to failure against a goal. With insight, analysis, and changes to your process, that can lead to hitting your goal.

It might even be what leads to discovering what helps your business launch past your initial goals. That all starts with setting goals in the first place to commit to understanding your business.

Managing Resources Effectively

While operating a business, the most fundamental rule is that cash flow is king. When you run out of cash flow or financing, you're out of business.

If you don't have any customers or any cash flows, if you don't consistently bring in revenue from your operation, then you don't have a business yet.

When starting a business, you will have to plan its finances in advance to control how you venture the startup's resources and manage its expenses along the roadmap to healthy, sustainable, growing profits.

If you try to give your startup too much runway you may not have the urgency to find high yield producing operations for your business. If you don't give it enough runway and use all the startup's budget before reaching sustainable profitability, it's game over.

Your business's financial plan will most likely contain financial statements with your business' balance sheet, assets and liabilities, expenses and revenues.

You can use just spreadsheet documents to compile all this information together or a combination of word documents or PDFs and spreadsheets.

You might have a periodic routine on your calendar for yourself or a business manager to check the dashboard for apps your business uses and update info on your spreadsheets.

As you begin to put your business plan into action— piecemeal as you develop it or whole-hog after an intensive development or incubator stage to produce a complete and detailed plan before engaging the market— you will have in mind some idea of your fixed and operating costs, an idea that becomes more complete with research and market interactions.

You've got a viable path forward for your business plan if you have the startup funds, time, effort, leverage, techniques, opportunities, whatever— to cover the fixed costs to get started and then the marginal costs of fulfilling orders and break into profitability before running below the key floor threshold of cash your business requires to continue operating profitably.

Measuring Marketing Success

The algorithms on large social media platforms with active user bases are constantly being requested by the users to display posts from accounts they follow that the algorithm guesses based on their activity that they will like to see the most when they visit the app and start scrolling.

Drilling down into all the aspects of the manager dashboard for your accounts and ad campaigns, you will see how many views and engagements your posts received, and how many click-throughs they got for posts that feature a link.

Every view is an audition with the user for the part of being their guy for whatever your business sells. Every engagement is feedback, every click-through is an opportunity to acquire a customer, and every sale is the most crucial positive feedback your business can get.

Some ways to measure your business's marketing success are to compare results across platforms, media types, campaigns, and across customer segments.

Your results may be markedly better in some platforms than others, in which case you may find you want to focus your marketing dollars there if the platform is large enough.

You may also find that your product and offer get the most engagements and sales when advertised through a certain media type. For example, you might find that a short video you or your ad creatives made gets outlier results, or that text ads with certain keywords work best, or that text and image ads with a hero shot of your great-looking product work best.

You may also find that certain campaigns outperform or underperform others. That may be due to the advertising creatives as with the above examples, or it could be different campaigns you run, to different markets with different offers and/or pricing, that bring in the most sales.

You may find certain tactics like aggressive selling vs. soft-selling, or certain calls-to-action (CTA) push the most prospects through your sales funnel to become another satisfied customer. That's why constantly thinking about your marketing and A/B testing theories to improve your business's numbers is crucial to success.

CONCLUSION

Recap of Key Points

That concludes "How to Write a Business Plan and What to Consider When Starting a Business." Thank you for reading all the way through.

Remember, your business plan is fundamentally an exercise for you and other key principals of your business to test and refine your business as a simulation, using as much real-world data as you can get, to learn your business as much as possible before committing the time, effort, and money to it that you'll learn it requires from making the plan.

After you've built that foundation, your business will begin to become more real as you guide it through advertising tests on controlled samples of the market and make refinements from what you learn.

As you keep detailed and organized notes and records of your business's trial runs and full-fledged campaigns with the winningest, most profitable models, you will find yourself writing a story about the market with enough detail and input from the market that it becomes true.

If your business is profitable and growing quickly, you may want to bring in partners for leverage to scale faster and ensure the business can handle the growth without losing quality or customer satisfaction.

You may in this event seek a business loan from a bank, or lending company, or financial institution, or you may want to seek equity funding and raise private seed capital or an angel investment.

In either case, you will want to update and polish your business plan. You may also want to condense your business plan into various presentable formats like a pitch deck, slide presentation, and professionally written word document.

Unless you've closed a deal to completely sell out your company, you're never really done business planning. In our dynamic, fast-paced, ever-changing world, with an accelerating growth of opportunities and techniques, ongoing market research and business planning is essentially to keep your business up-to-date and current.

That way you can continually reassess and revise your business's strengths, weaknesses, opportunities, and threats, and what your business does about the landscape of vertical and horizontal competition.

You can identify ways your business could expand or pivot, areas your business is leaving money on the table, and ways and means to lower your business's time and cost expenditures. A constantly adapting business could evolve rapidly enough to become a very big fish in the oceanic digital marketplace.

Advertisement: When you're serious about starting your business, you will probably need to start an LLC, a Limited Liability Company. That protects your personal and household finances and legal status from liabilities that arise from the operation of your business.

If you enjoyed reading "How to Write A Business Plan and What to Consider When Starting A Business," please consider reading "A Beginners Guide to Properly Form and Manage an LLC. Strategies to Maximize Asset Protection, Tax Breaks and Save Legal Fees."

Book #3

Marketing and Sales for Business Owners

Introduction

Many companies have forgotten they sell to actual people. Humans care about the entire experience, not just the marketing or sales or service. To really win in the modern age, you must solve for humans.
Dharmesh Shah

Gone are the days when marketing a business meant throwing messages in a customer's face, such as:

"What are you waiting for? Buy now!"

"The best product you have ever seen in your life!"

"Let us take care of all your household needs!"

It made sense back then why businesses would use every opportunity to unashamedly sell their brands. Communication channels were limited to only a few (i.e., radio, TV, and the newspaper), and they weren't sure whether their target audience would see their messages or not.

But over time, and with vast technological improvements, the world of marketing became more sophisticated—and so did the average customer. It is rare to find businesses that market themselves in one big sales pitch. This is because customers have become weary of advertising where the motive is to sell products or services.

Telling a modern-day customer to "Buy now!" won't have the same effect as it did decades ago, simply because there is no need that is being solved. What makes a customer want to open their wallet and purchase a product or service is knowing that they are fulfilling one of their needs.

In other words, it isn't so much about the product or service itself, but about how it solves a problem or responds to a core need. Therefore, to produce successful marketing initiatives, businesses need to learn how to identify their customers' needs and help solve them through products or services.

Every marketing department creates a marketing plan. But how relevant and effective is that plan? Does it focus on a specific audience? Has it understood the audience's needs and preferences? And have the right channels been selected to engage with them?

These are just some of the questions that will be explored and answered throughout the book. Over the course of eight chapters, we will break down what a modern marketing plan consists of, metrics to measure its effectiveness, and the components of building and automating a strong brand. After finishing this book, you will walk away with practical marketing tools to kickstart your next campaign!

CHAPTER 1

Traditional vs Modern Marketing

Ignoring online marketing is like opening a business but not telling anyone.
KB Marketing Agency

What Is Traditional Marketing?

Traditional marketing is not a new concept. Before the internet, marketing existed offline through mediums like the newspaper, magazines, radio, and TV. Since it existed offline, and customers had no way of reaching out and engaging with businesses, marketing was purely focused on selling products and services—not necessarily building relationships.

Examples of some of the offline tactics used to promote businesses include:

- **Handouts:** Printed flyers or pamphlets that are used to share information about a business, such as a business overview, product offerings, contact details, and special offers.

- **Billboards:** Large boards that are installed along major intersections or highways, which display company graphics. They are mostly used when launching new products into the markets.

- **Direct mail:** Posted newsletters, postcards, or magazines that are usually sent to members of a specific club or group created by a company. For example, platinum card members of a prestigious bank might be added to the mailing list to receive monthly printed material.

- **Broadcasting:** Advertising through radio or TV channels to a large or niche audience. Broadcasting adverts seek to educate target audiences about the products and services—or special promotions—a business is offering.

- **Cold calling:** Advertising a business's products or service by making phone calls to potential customers, and persuading them to make a purchase or sign up for special offers while they are on the line.

The reason why traditional marketing has stood the test of time is because of how effective it can be in promoting a business. Many audiences are familiar with printed ads or radio broadcasts, and using these tactics may give your business credibility. Traditional marketing can also reach niche audiences, who may not have a strong online presence (i.e., consumers who live in small towns), or who may be loyal to these mediums (i.e., consumers who listen to a certain radio station every morning or who collect magazines).

The downside with traditional marketing is that it promotes one-way communication between the business and its customers. Nowadays, this strategy can come across as inauthentic or "salesy." Customers want to be able to ask questions and interact with businesses throughout the sales journey. Additionally, traditional marketing makes measuring campaign objectives difficult. It is not easy to track how many potential customers were reached, and of those, how many continued on the sales journey.

What Is Modern Marketing?

With the advancement of technology, digital marketing channels were introduced. Their job was to fulfill one purpose, which is to help businesses become more customer-centric. Instead of the traditional one-way advertising, businesses could engage with members of its target audience in real-time, and respond to their unique needs and desires.

Modern marketing is advertising pushed over the internet. Whatever you would have originally printed on paper, you can distribute as a social media post, blog article, or email newsletter. Similar to traditional marketing, there are different tactics you can adopt to advertise online, such as:

- **Internet adverts:** Paid posts or banners that are placed on search engines like Google or social media platforms like Facebook or Instagram.

- **Email marketing:** Electronic newsletters sent to a curated mailing list to share notices and updates on business offerings and promotions.

- **E-commerce marketing:** Advertising physical or digital products on an online marketplace like eBay, Etsy, or Facebook Marketplace.

- **E-learning:** Sharing instructional or technical knowledge, via tools like online courses or webinars, to educate members of your target audience.

- **Content marketing:** Advertising business products or services through search engine optimized (SEO) articles.

Digital marketing has grown in popularity over the years. According to research, 68% of startup businesses use at least one modern marketing tool (Capers, 2021). So, what exactly are the advantages of investing in this type of marketing strategy?

One of the benefits of modern marketing is extended reach. With just one paid social media advert, you can reach customers in different states or countries. Or, if your business caters to a niche audience, you can customize your advertising selection criteria to only show your posts to people who match your customer profile—down to the musical bands they listen to!

Another benefit is affordability. For startup businesses that are tight on budget, advertising online can be virtually free (except if you desire to invest money behind your ads). Plus, there are plenty of graphic design software that offer free social media post templates to choose from. With a bit of creativity, you can produce quality business ads without the need to outsource help.

As attractive as modern marketing is, it has its drawbacks. For instance, since you will be advertising online, you will need to have basic knowledge on how to navigate online platforms, leverage tools like SEO, measure and interpret website or social media analytics, and so on.

Another drawback is the increased competition that businesses are met with online. For startups, it can be difficult to sell products or services when you are up against established businesses with larger marketing budgets. To overcome this particular challenge, you will need to create a compelling brand (more on how to do that later in the book).

The Verdict: Traditional or Modern Marketing?

Many businesses feel pressured to choose between traditional or modern marketing. The truth is that both strategies are effective depending on a few factors, such as:

- **Budget:** How much money do you have to advertise your business? Traditional marketing normally works when a business has a large budget because sending hundreds of postcards, or booking a slot on radio can be really expensive.

- **Goals:** Think carefully about your marketing goals. For instance, are you launching your business, seeking to increase awareness, or promoting a special? Handing out flyers at a local shopping mall can be a great tactic during a launch, but for ongoing awareness or time-sensitive promotions, social media marketing may be more effective.

- **Target audience:** What marketing channels does your target audience use? Depending on their age, education, lifestyle, and habits, you may be more successful using traditional or modern tools. For example, older generations may prefer reading a newspaper than reading an online article, so newspaper ads would be highly effective.

- **Industry:** Lastly, the industry that you are competing in can also determine what marketing tactics you use. Generally, businesses in retail, food, tourism, or electronic goods and services would benefit from leveraging modern technological tools to reach target audiences. This is because their products and services are appropriate to be advertised online. This wouldn't be the case for businesses in mining or manufacturing.

Therefore, there isn't a right or wrong way of marketing your business. The aim is to understand what you stand for, where your target audience can be found, and the best ways to get your messages out there.

CHAPTER 2

Understand Your Market

Build something 100 people love, not something 1 million people kind of like.
Brian Chesky

Identifying Your Target Audience

A target audience is a group of consumers who you have identified as being the most appropriate people to market your products and services. Since most modern businesses specialize, their offerings solve problems for specific people. A good example is a vegan frozen foods company whose products would be appealing to customers that love:

- vegan food

- frozen food

- convenient cooking

- fresh box meals

Identifying your target audience should ideally be one of the first things you do when creating a marketing plan. Not only can finding your audience cut your marketing costs, it can also help you find the right offline and online channels, and sell your business using visuals, symbols, and messages that would attract your ideal customers.

On a foundational level, you can identify your target audience by their demographics. This would entail finding out the following information about your chosen audience:

- age

- gender

- location

- marital status

- employment

- income bracket

- socio-economic status

- educational history

In order to gain real insights, it is important to conduct market research to investigate how large your target audience is, and whether there are enough people who would find your products or services desirable. Nowadays, you don't need to purchase marketing reports or surveys to learn more about your target audience. You can find relevant information by going onto industry or journal websites, or downloading free market research analysis documents.

Questions to Explore Your Target Audience

When conducting your research, it can help to think of your target audience as a real human being who has a particular problem that your business can solve. Take an inside look into that individual's life and get to know them better—specifically in what ways they would be exposed to your business.

Below are a few guiding questions that you can explore, as you identify your target audience (record your responses on the line space provided or in a separate document):

1. What does your audience do for work?

This question can answer a lot of questions about how to market your business to the audience. For instance, if your target audience has a traditional 9-to-5 job, they may have a lot of restrictions on their time. Selling convenience is the best way to get their attention because they want products and services that free up their time. Understanding what your audience does for work can also help you gauge which times of the day or week to post content or run specials.

Record your research findings below:

_____

_____

_____

_____

_____

2. What kind of lifestyle does your audience live?

Knowing what kind of lifestyle your audience lives can help you better understand their interests, passions, and personality. Moreover, you can learn more about what products or services they like or dislike, and whether they apply certain philosophies when it comes to supporting businesses. For example, a customer who is environmentally conscious cares about how much energy and materials businesses use to manufacture goods.

Record your research findings below:

_____

_____

_____

_____

_____

3. What does your audience think?

Customers make purchasing decisions based on preexisting beliefs, values, and attitudes. When you understand what and how your audience thinks, you can make better marketing decisions, such as knowing what messages might get the best reactions from them, or knowing how to position yourself as a positive business in their lives. Since this question requires you to gather perceptions, it is recommended to conduct a survey with a few members of your target audience.

Record your survey results below:

_____
_____
_____
_____
_____

4. How does your audience communicate?

Another key insight is knowing how your audience communicates. On a basic level, this entails understanding the tools they use to keep in touch with others. For example, are they mostly on their phones or laptops? Do they prefer face-to-face interactions (suitable for traditional marketing) or online interactions (suitable for digital marketing)? Thereafter, you can explore which platforms they prefer, how many times per week they login, how long they stay online, and other communication behaviors like whether they engage with businesses via direct messages (DM), leave product or business reviews, or often recommend businesses to their personal network.

Record your research findings below:

_____
_____
_____
_____
_____

5. What challenges is your audience facing?

Businesses exist to solve consumer needs. It is important to figure out what particular challenges your audience is facing that you can assist with. In other words, you must find a gap that your products or services can fill in their lives. One way to learn about your audience's challenges is to perform what is known as social media listening. It involves searching for keywords related to your business, competitors, current affairs, lifestyle choices, and other general topics that might reveal obstacles. Another option is to complete a survey with members of your target audience and ask about some of their work, health, family, lifestyle, or relationship challenges.

Record your research findings below:

_____
_____
_____
_____
_____

Audience Segmentation

Once you have identified your target audience, you can complete the segmentation process. Target audience segmentation refers to using the data collected about a specific audience to divide consumers into smaller groups based on similar characteristics. Completing this process helps you customize messages to appeal to the interests of each segment. You can also develop campaigns tailored for each segment, instead of pushing one generic campaign that doesn't appeal to any particular group.

There are various ways to "split" your target audience and create smaller groups. The best way is to divide the groups based on different attributes, such as:

- **Demographics**: Group audiences based on their age, gender, income, educational history, socio-economic status, or geographical location. For example, you might show store-based promotions to audiences situated within a few miles from the retail store.

- **Lifestyle factors:** Group audiences based on their interests, hobbies, beliefs, and attitudes. For example, if you are selling a recipe book, you might target members of your target audience who follow food or cooking hashtags on social media, or those who are homemakers.

- **Behaviors:** Group audiences based on their purchasing behaviors, or the common ways they interact with your business or products. For example, a customer who makes purchases on a weekly or monthly basis won't need to see messages encouraging them to return.

- **Buyer's journey:** Group audiences based on where they are on the buyer's journey (e.g., whether they are at the awareness, consideration, or decision-making stage). For example, customers who are still at the awareness stage desire to learn more about the business and its offerings, whereas those who are ready to make a decision may need an incentive, like a discount code, to complete the transaction.

If you are selling niche products or services, you may want to create additional segments within larger segments. For example, if you are marketing your latest online course about stock marketing investing, you can create a smaller segment under "Demographics" which targets males, aged 28–45, who live in New York City, and work as investment bankers or finance managers. The more customized your segments are, the more targeted your messages will be.

After coming up with different target audience segments, you can create customer personas. For each segment, write down a detailed description of the ideal customer. Profile each customer as though it were somebody you knew. These customer personas will help you determine the style, tone, and feel of your messages whenever you are marketing to that specific group.

CHAPTER 3

Develop a Marketing Strategy

**The attention economy is not growing, which means that we have to
grab the attention that someone else has today.**
Brent Leary

What Is a Marketing Strategy?

A marketing strategy is a detailed plan that explains how you are going
to entice the right customers to purchase your goods or services. An
effective marketing strategy won't merely include tactics. It will also lay
out the business's marketing goals and objectives, unique value
proposition, information about the target audience, and the four Ps of
marketing (product, price, place, and promotion).

The information required to put together a marketing strategy is
collected from extensive market research. Without relevant and factual
data, you won't have a clear idea of who your customers are, where you
can find them, and the best ways to position yourself as a business.
There are various tools you can use to conduct market research, which
include:

- **Surveys:** Create free surveys or questionnaires and distribute
  them on your website, via email, or on your social media pages.
  Surveys are useful for gathering target audience insights, which
  may not be easily found online.

- **Blogs and social networks:** If you are looking for qualitative
  research that allows you to learn more about human experiences
  that can't be put into numbers, then you can visit relevant blogs

or social media accounts that explore topics or interests your audience cares about.

- **Pew Research Center:** This non-profit organization conducts and distributes free research studies across a range of domains, including US politics and policy, social media trends and demographics, technology and the internet, and public opinion polling, to name a few.

- **US Census Business Bureau:** This website shares free market research that can help you identify members of your target audience. Some of the data you will find offers the latest trends in the economy, population size and growth, labor market statistics, income statistics, and industry trends in North America.

A marketing strategy can often be confused with a marketing plan. The main difference between these two elements is that the marketing strategy provides an explanation of the business goals and certain criteria that need to be met in order to achieve those goals. On the other hand, the marketing plan is a document that is constantly updated to outline the marketing activities the business is working on during each quarter or year.

Typically, a marketing strategy will be designed to live longer than a marketing plan because it contains the long-term vision of the company's value proposition, brand, and approach to attracting customers. The strategy will also inform the marketing team's initiatives and the various campaigns or activities they choose to execute.

To make a practical illustration, the marketing strategy for your business may be to position yourself as a customer-centric brand that offers unbeatable low prices. Your marketing plan would explore the logistical details and initiatives that would need to be carried out to convey that message and attract the right customers. Some of these initiatives might include offering frequent sales or discounts, rewarding customers with coupon codes for regularly visiting your store, or introducing a loyalty program that allows customers to save extra money.

There are four elements that you will need to consider when creating your marketing strategy: goals and objectives, unique value proposition, finding the right marketing mix, and measuring the effectiveness of your marketing strategy. The sections below will take an in-depth look into each element and easy steps to get started.

Identify Your Marketing Goals and Objectives

Marketing objectives are the clear, measurable, achievable, and time-bound goals that your team strives to accomplish within a period of time. Creating marketing goals and objectives is not the same as traditional goal-setting. Above and beyond determining what you need to do, marketing goals and objectives tell you exactly how to do it. This leaves out a lot of guesswork and saves your team time when implementing the strategy.

Another interesting distinction between marketing goals and objectives and traditional goal-setting is that the former communicates the "why" behind your marketing efforts. Sharing the purpose of your business must be interwoven in the process of attracting the right customers. Doing so not only helps customers resonate with your business, but it can also strengthen the relationships you form.

You can think of marketing goals and objectives as being the "anchor" that grounds all of your marketing activities. As such, these goals and objectives must be aspirational enough to allow room for creative exploration. The truth is there are hundreds of tactics that can help you entice customers, but not every tactic is aligned with your business's core values and purpose. Having this anchor serves as a reminder of what you stand for and the kind of impact you desire to make in your customers' lives.

There is a difference between a goal and an objective. The goal is usually the vision, or bigger picture, that you hope to achieve. Since it is abstract, it is supposed to provide inspiration and a sense of direction. Objectives are the actionable steps that you set out to achieve your goal. These are designed to be specific, practical, and achievable within a specific time frame.

Before establishing objectives, you will need to define your marketing goal. Take a moment to think about the purpose behind marketing your business and what you hope to achieve. Below are a few questions to get you thinking:

1. What does success look like for your business? What do you hope to achieve?

_____

_____

_____

_____

_____

2. What is the big "why" behind what you hope to achieve?

_____

_____

_____

_____

_____

3. What problems have you identified that have led you to this point? Why is it important for these problems to be solved?

_____

_____

_____

_____

_____

In the space below, write down a rough draft of your marketing goal. You are welcome to refine the goal as many times as you like.

_____

_____

_____

_____

_____

The next step is to create objectives that help you achieve your goal. The simplest framework to use when creating objectives is SMART goal-setting. SMART is an acronym that stands for "specific, measurable, attainable, relevant, and time-bound." Using this framework will help you define the various action steps you are going to take.

Below is a brief overview on how to use the SMART goal-setting framework:

- **Specific:** Identify a specific marketing metric you want to improve, such as getting more foot traffic on your website or increasing brand awareness.

- **Measurable:** Find ways to quantify your success by setting percentage targets or aiming for a certain number of monthly visitors on your page.

- **Attainable:** Look back at your metric and measurements and ask yourself whether what you are aiming for is attainable. For example, have you set a metric that is realistic for the size of your business and the industry you are competing in?

- **Relevant:** Determine whether your objective is aligned with your marketing goal and overall mission of the company, or trends within your industry.

- **Time-bound:** Set a realistic time frame to achieve your objective. Bear in mind that the more time you give yourself, the more vulnerable you are to procrastination or paralysis by over-analysis.

An example of a SMART objective would be to increase foot traffic to your website by 20% each month, for the duration of a year. The goal backing this objective may have been getting more people to visit your online store so that you can increase online sales.

This objective is measurable because your target is set at 20%-foot traffic increase on a monthly basis. It is attainable because perhaps last year you were able to achieve a 15% increase month-on-month. It is relevant because it aligns with your marketing goal of increasing online sales in your store. And lastly, it is time-bound because you are working on a 12-month time frame.

Practice setting SMART objectives that align with your goals below.

_____

_____

_____

_____

_____

_____

_____

_____

Craft Your Unique Value Proposition

A unique value proposition (UVP) is a statement that communicates why your business is different from the rest, and how customers can benefit from purchasing your products or services. This statement is often posted in highly visible locations, like your social media bio or the homepage of your website, so that customers are clear about what they can expect when doing business with you.

The UVP is the persuasive element that helps customers choose you over competitors. Depending on how saturated your industry is, this simple yet impactful statement can give you a dominant position in the minds of potential customers. Not only are you selling the benefits of your offerings, but you are also selling the unique buying experience that only you can provide.

Most people mistakenly confuse a UVP with a motto or slogan; however, it is more than that. A motto or slogan is a creative catchphrase that makes the brand memorable. It isn't designed to promote the business or its offerings. The UVP helps consumers distinguish between one brand from another. It highlights the main benefits of a particular business and how it promises to make the customers' lives simpler, healthier, or more convenient.

Despite the fact that the UVP is a single sentence or two, crafting one can be very tricky. Many businesses fall into the trap of putting together a collection of catchy words, which make the sentence sound generic and inauthentic. Think of your UVP as the first impression you make to potential customers. Be mindful of how you represent your business and what you stand for. Below are a few things to consider before creating your statement:

- Be mindful of not sounding like other existing businesses. Keep your tone and language unique to your brand identity.

- Avoid mentioning benefits that are common amongst businesses in your industry. Think carefully about the unique experiences you can offer.

- Keep your sentences simple and easy to follow. When customers read the UVP, you want them to be able to envision the pleasant experience of shopping with you.

- Read the statement over and over again in the voice and perspective of each customer persona. Imagine how each customer will read and interpret the statement, and whether they will be driven to support your business.

When you are ready to craft your UVP, grab a pen and follow these simple steps:

1. Make a list of the products or services you offer.

_____

_____

_____

_____

_____

2. For each product or service, make a list of benefits to customers. Ensure that the benefits you list are genuine and guaranteed.

_____

_____

_____

_____

_____

3. Look at the list above and remove the benefits your competitors also offer. Write down the revised list below.

_____

_____

_____

_____

_____

4. Write down the first draft of your UVP. Start out by mentioning what your business is about and the benefits of your products or services. Note that this first draft may be unusually long (consisting of a few sentences), but this is expected.

_____

_____

_____

_____

_____

5. From the statement above, remove words or sentences that are "general" or something you would find inside a business plan. You can also remove repetitive words or phrases that are confusing like

"We take care of your pets, so you don't have to." Rewrite the UVP below.

_____

_____

_____

_____

_____

6. Read the UVP to yourself and think about each customer that your business serves. Does the UVP solve their problems? Will it make them desire to do business with you? Edit your UVP once more, so that it reflects the interests of your customers.

_____

_____

_____

_____

_____

As you may have realized, crafting a UVP requires several drafts. Continue to refine your sentence to ensure you make the best first impression. It is also important to think back to your marketing goals and objectives and determine whether your UVP effectively sells your business.

To inspire you, here are examples of powerful UVPs created by companies who have become household names (Omniconvert, 2023):

- Walmart: Save money. Live better.

- FedEx: When it absolutely, positively has to be there overnight.

- M&Ms: Melt in your mouth, not in your hand.

- Domino's Pizza: A hot pizza delivered in less than 30 minutes or it's free.

- iPod: 1,000 songs in your pocket.

- VISA: Everywhere you want to be.

Compile the Right Marketing Mix

Your product or service is the "leading lady" in your business. However, no matter how amazing the product or service is, it cannot sell itself. This is where the marketing mix comes in. Every marketing strategy includes a marketing mix, which is a list of elements that help you effectively market your business. How you define each element will change depending on industry trends, customer needs, business growth, and so on.

The term "marketing mix" was coined by Harvard Graduate School researcher, Neil Borden in the 1950s, but popularized a decade later by marketing professor, E. Jerome McCarthy, who came up with the four Ps of marketing (i.e., product, price, place, and promotion) to describe the various elements of the marketing mix (Doxee, 2020). Several decades later, researchers Mary Bitner and Bernard Booms added three more elements to the marketing mix to accommodate businesses that were selling services, instead of only products.

This resulted in what we know today as the "7 Ps of marketing," which are defined as follows:

1. Product

The point of marketing your business is to sell a physical or digital product. This can be a challenge when you are competing in a saturated industry full of many similar products, with little room to differentiate yours. To effectively market your product, you will need to focus on what makes it unique, such as the distinct features, packaging, aesthetics, quality, or usefulness it offers.

You can also find ways to enhance your product by improving your branding, customer service, delivery process, return policy, warranty policy, and product sophistication (e.g., leveraging technological tools to make your product smarter).

2. Price

The price point of your product is what ultimately sells your product, apart from its features. To get the pricing right, you will need to create a pricing strategy that considers your competitor's pricing, what your target audience can afford, cost of producing the product, and the profit margins you hope to make from selling each product.

Another consideration to make is whether you have positioned yourself as a premium or affordable brand. These categories also help to create a price range that you can work from. Note that the price you set should reflect trends and shifts in the market, and will therefore change whenever you are confronted with different variables, such as inflation or fuel hikes.

3. Place

In the 50s and 60s, many businesses had a physical store, which was the "place" of operation. However, nowadays, businesses can be situated and operate online. Nevertheless, there will still be a distribution model that every business follows, regardless of their location. You have the task of refining your distribution model to offer as much convenience for customers as possible. If you are operating a physical store, think of how you can design your shop-front window to invite customers, or where to place products around the store for optimum visibility.

If you are operating an online store, think about the layout of your website, user experience, and how quick it is to search for items and complete the checkout process. Moreover, your customer service team will play a huge role in helping customers transact, online or in a physical store. Ensure that you have a strategy for how your team interacts with and assists customers.

4. Promotion

Promotion is typically what we refer to as advertising. Knowing how and where to promote your products or services can increase the chances of reaching your ideal customers. Products that aren't advertised enough, or in the correct channels, go unnoticed. Factors like price and product placement may also influence customers' purchasing decisions.

In the first chapter, we looked at both traditional and modern marketing tactics that can help you promote business offerings. When creating your promotion strategy, you would need to consider which tactics work best for your business. You can also have a look at which platforms your competitors are promoting their products or services on, and the various tactics they are using.

5. People

A certain individual, team, or agency must be in charge of managing and measuring your marketing initiatives. If you are a small business, you may be the person responsible for creating the strategy and executing your marketing objectives. Alternatively, you can hire a third-party agency or social media coordinator to assist you with specific tasks. To ensure the right people are hired, make sure that your team understands your brand, vision, and strategy, and that they have the necessary skills and training to perform their duties.

6. Process

Marketing is the front-end, business processes are the back-end. In order to achieve a smooth and seamless execution of your marketing strategy, you will need to find ways to simplify your processes. For example, consider how many steps it takes customers to sign up on your website, fulfill orders, return goods, post reviews, and receive communication from your business. Moreover, consider how quickly it takes customers to navigate your website or find answers to their burning questions. When your processes are complicated or take too long, customers may be less motivated to continue on the sales journey.

7. Physical evidence

Lastly, it is important to consider the tangible business identifiers that influence public perception. These may include elements like your logo and branding, product packaging, business cards, website, physical store, or social media pages. In most cases, potential customers will interact with these elements before finding out more about your business. You can improve the physical evidence of your business by being clear about who you are and how you desire to be perceived by other customers or businesses.

If you already have a marketing mix, but aren't getting the results you are looking for, you may need to go back to the drawing board. Refer back to your marketing goals and objectives and figure out what else is missing from your mix that can improve your marketing methods. You may also need to ask yourself questions like: Am I targeting the right customers? Am I promoting my business on the right channels? Is my pricing competitive? And, in what ways can I improve my distribution model?

Measure the Effectiveness of Your Strategy

To assess the effectiveness of your marketing strategy, you will need to quantify the results using a few marketing metrics. The numbers will indicate whether you are achieving your objectives or not. For example, if your objective was to increase the number of sales from email newsletters, you would need to measure the conversion rate (the percentage of people who decide to make a purchase after being offered something).

Keep in mind that business accounts on social media platforms or blogs offer general statistics about the performance of your posts and how many people have visited your page within a certain time period (typically in the space of a week). For example, you may get shown the number of clicks on a post, the engagement rate, or how often people discovered your post on their feeds.

These metrics are useful; however, they won't necessarily show you how effective your marketing strategy is. For example, if 200 people "like" a post, you won't be able to tell how many of them purchased the product you were promoting. These metrics are good to use when assessing the effectiveness of a post or campaign you are running at the moment.

Below are common metrics to calculate when determining the effectiveness of your marketing strategy:

1. Sales growth

Sales growth measures the changes in revenue over a period of time. For instance, you can compare the sales growth on a month-by-month basis, at the beginning and end of a campaign, or whenever you offer sales discounts. To measure sales growth, you can look at the total revenue volume or number of products or services sold within a time frame.

2. Profit variance

Profit variance helps you determine whether you are making a return on investment (ROI) within a specific time period. The factors that affect profitability are increased expenses, such as higher than normal material or marketing costs. If your revenue stays the same each month, but your material or marketing costs increase, then you are making less profit.

3. New customer volume

New customer volume measures the total number of new customers over a period of time. If one of your objectives is to serve a certain number of customers every month, this metric can help you determine if you are reaching the specified target. The metric can also come in handy when you are running a promotion and want to measure how many new customers you acquired at the end of the period.

4. Lifetime customer value

Ideally, you want new customers to become returning customers. Measuring the lifetime customer value helps you assess how many existing customers make continuous purchases. To calculate this metric, multiply the average number of purchases made by returning customers with the average total value of the purchases. You can track the lifetime customer value over a quarterly, bi-annual, or annual basis. The higher the value, the more stable your revenue streams.

5. Conversion rate

Conversation rate measures how many people follow through when presented with a call-t0-action, like signing up to the newsletter, taking a free trial, or using a discount code. You can calculate this metric by taking the number of conversions over a period of time, divided by the number of advert or post interactions during the same period.

Analytical tools like Web trends and Google Analytics are beginner-friendly and great to use when measuring different metrics. They provide you with plenty of statistics about the number, type, and frequency of visitors that access your website, as well as data related to the activities of website users, like how they navigate your website, which pages they spend most of their time on, and what actions they typically take.

We have discussed the four elements that are necessary components of a marketing strategy. These include identifying your marketing goal and objectives, crafting a unique value proposition, compiling the right marketing mix, and measuring the effectiveness of your strategy. Extensive market research is required when completing each element of your strategy to ensure that you make decisions based on current and relevant data.

CHAPTER 4

Create Compelling Content

If your stories are all about your products and services, that's not storytelling. It's a brochure. Give yourself permission to make the story bigger.
Jay Baer

What Is Content Marketing?

Content marketing is a type of marketing strategy that is used by businesses to increase brand awareness and keep the audience engaged. Different tools, including articles, videos, podcasts, and photographs, are used to distribute relevant information to existing and potential customers.

Nowadays, it is becoming normal for every business with an online presence to produce content. This is because sharing content has been found to be effective in building and nurturing relationships with customers. Research has shown businesses with blogs get 67% more leads than those that don't have blogs, and 82% of consumers feel more positive about a business after reading curated content (Demand Metric, 2019).

When done correctly, content marketing can offer your business many benefits, such as:

- **Increasing online visibility:** By sharing custom content, you can establish a presence online and get your business in front of your target audience. Being discoverable online can also increase your business credibility and reputation.

- **Receiving more leads:** When your content includes a call-to-action, you can direct traffic to various channels, like your website or online store. Plus, using content to direct traffic makes measuring your campaigns or marketing initiatives a lot easier.

- **Building customer loyalty:** When the content you are sharing is engaging, your business will be top of mind. Whenever customers are looking for business or product-related information, they are more likely to visit your online channels. In the long run, they may see your business as a reliable source of information, and this can increase loyalty.

During the different stages of the sales journey (i.e., awareness, consideration, and decision-making stages), you have an opportunity to share custom content that helps customers learn more about your business, and eventually make a purchase. Below is an example of the kinds of content pieces you would produce and distribute at each stage:

- **Awareness:** At this stage, customers are still getting to know your business and your UVP. The type of content you share should focus on brand awareness, highlighting benefits of your products or services, and showing customers how you can help them solve problems. The best formats for content during this stage are articles, newsletters, eBooks, and tutorials.

- **Consideration:** At this stage, customers are familiar with your business and are beginning to contemplate making a purchase. The type of content you share should be both educational and promotional. For example, you can zero in on the various products and highlight the features, or speak about aspects of your business you are proud of, such as your overnight delivery process. Examples of types of content that work well during this stage are testimonials, case studies, and how-to videos.

- **Decision-making:** At this stage, customers are close to making a sale, but need an extra push to get over the resistance. Promotional content offering discount codes or time-based offers are a great way to motivate customers to buy. You can also focus on creating content to address customer questions and concerns. Examples of content formats that are suitable during this stage are frequently asked questions (FAQs), user-generated content, free buyer's manuals, and promotional emails.

The goal of a good content marketing strategy is to create the right content, for the right platforms or channels, at the right time.

The Importance of Storytelling in Content Marketing

Stories are tools that our minds use to interpret information. When we hear stories, we are able to tap into our imaginations and understand the meaning behind words and symbols. In ancient times, folktales were told to document and make sense of the experiences of a particular tribe or community of people; and within religious communities, parables or moral stories were often told as a way of teaching values and principles.

What has made storytelling so effective throughout history is the way in which stories modify human behavior without necessarily forcing change. The active use of imagination allows for reflection and empathy, which causes people to desire taking action. When creating content, businesses can use storytelling to positively influence consumer behavior and inspire them to take action.

Below are a few ways that storytelling can enhance content marketing:

1. Making the brand memorable

Consumers are bombarded with millions of ads on a daily basis. If the content doesn't provide a release of dopamine within the first few seconds of engagement, they are more likely to keep scrolling. Telling stories gets people to stop and read or listen to what you have to say. Your messages stand out from the crowd because nobody else can tell a story in the same way as your business.

2. Humanizing the business

Storytelling can help businesses build more relatable brands that capture the human experience. By telling a story about the challenges experienced in everyday life, for example, your business can connect to customers on an emotional level. Good stories can also lead to brand loyalty and advocacy. For instance, a customer who feels seen and heard by your business may recommend your products or services to their network.

3. Motivating action

Stories personally affect those who read or listen to them. When told correctly, they have the power to stir emotions and lead to decision-making. As such, when telling stories through your content, be sure to add a call-to-action to influence the customer's next steps.

There are many different ways to tell stories through content marketing. To add more structure to the element of storytelling, marketers have created techniques that inform how stories should be told for best results. Three of these techniques include:

AIDA Technique

AIDA stands for "attention, interest, desire, and action." This technique is one of the traditional methods of telling stories through content marketing. Below are the steps to practice the technique:

- **Attention:** Grab the customer's attention within the first seconds of engaging with your content by making a bold statement, mentioning shocking statistics, telling an unusual story, or asking an emotional or provocative question like "Do you want to drop 20 pounds in three months?"

- **Interest:** The next task will be to keep the customer engaged by getting to the "heart" of your story. What's important is having a powerful message to share and using the most effective medium (i.e., article, video, infographic) to develop the story.

- **Desire:** To motivate a customer to support your business, they need to feel a desire to associate themselves with your brand. You can create desire by selling your UVP or being deliberate about promoting the experience of working with you, or joining your community.

- **Action:** The final step is the easiest—getting your customer to take action. If you have done a good job at developing your story, they will naturally feel a sense of urgency to transact or complete the prescribed call-to-action.

The 4P Model

The 4P model is similar to AIDA, except it gives you more opportunity to present a compelling story. The four stages of the model include:

- **Promise:** Start out by making a promise to the customer to grab their attention. This could be a promise about how you can solve their problems. Keep the promise realistic so that people are driven to believe you. For example, you might say, "Our weight loss program is designed specifically for your body and diet."

- **Picture:** The next step is to encourage the customer to visualize the positive experience of doing business with you. Strong copywriting skills, with the use of emotive language, can help you take the customer on a journey from where they are now to where they could be if they invested in your product or service.

- **Proof:** The customer may be persuaded by the promise and picture; however, what gets them to commit is seeing the facts or evidence of the effectiveness of your products or services. Here again, you have an opportunity to tell stories about how your offerings have positively impacted the lives of existing customers. You can share testimonials, case studies, or user-generated content to gain trust and credibility.

- **Push:** The final step is to direct the customer toward a specific end goal. Think about what you would like them to do after engaging with your content. Add the most appropriate call-to-action to help them make a sale.

"Before-After-Bridge" Technique

The before-after-bridge technique takes readers through three stages. At first, they are presented with a challenging situation, then asked to visualize the best possible outcome, before being introduced to the value and offerings of the business. Below are the steps to implement the before-after-bridge technique:

- **Before:** Describe an existing problem, the customer is facing. Use emotive language to appeal to create a moment of self-reflection. Ideally, the customer should be able to see themselves in the story and understand the impact of their situation.

- **After:** The next step is to get the customer to dream about life after overcoming their problem. Once again, emotive language can help you capture the positive outcome you intend on helping customers achieve. This part of your story should feel lighter, happier, and more vibrant than the first part.

- **Bridge:** Bring the focus back to your business and your offerings. Introduce the particular products or services that might help customers achieve the desired end goal. Highlight the features and benefits of the offerings, and ensure they align with the aspirational outcome you described above.

Three Elements of a Powerful Marketing Story

The toughest part about creating content isn't telling a story, but instead figuring out what story to tell. When you have a message and are ready to draft a marketing story, incorporate these seven elements:

Goal

The first step is to be clear on what you hope to achieve with your story. This will inform the type of story you choose to tell, as well as how you deliver it. A few examples of worthy goals include:

- selling a product or service

- introducing the business

- starting a discussion

- celebrating a milestone

- educating the customer

Another important consideration to make when deciding on your goal is the intention behind telling this particular story. In other words, what do you hope customers take away from the story? What impact do you want to make? How do you want them to act after engaging with your story?

Structure

Now that you have clarified your goal, the next step is to choose the structure of your story. Depending on what you hope to achieve, you can create a story that follows one of these structures:

- **Business story:** Tell a story about your organization: who you are, what you stand for, the products or services you offer, and how you can help customers solve specific problems. If you want to humanize your business, you can tell stories of your personal victories, failures, and goals you are working toward.

- **Knowledge-based story:** Position yourself as a thought leader by telling a story that educates customers. You can share tips, strategies, tutorials, research, or advice that can help them make better decisions.

- **Action-based story:** Tell a story about the decisions you have made to get to where you are today, or the actions that customers can take to improve their lives. What makes this story compelling is that it has an element of knowledge, but is aimed at motivating customers.

- **Value-based story:** Identify values that your business shares with members of your community, then tell a story that highlights these values. For instance, you might share a story about social causes your business supports, the efforts you are making to reduce your carbon footprint, how you treat your employees, or customer testimonials that show your commitment to quality service.

Note that it is possible to combine structures, such as creating a story about your business that is also value-driven. The structure you choose all depends on your goal and the message you desire customers to walk away with.

Call-to-Action

Every good story includes a call-to-action. This can be a simple instruction that informs customers of the next steps. Customers don't want to have to figure out on their own what to do with the information you have given them. Including a call-to-action shortens the deliberation process and leads them toward the solution. Examples of call-to-actions include:

- Sign up.

- Subscribe.

- Donate.

- Click here.

- Buy now and get 30% off.

- Visit our website for more details.

- Start your free trial today.

When creating your call-to-action, remember to make a clear command. It isn't considered rude to tell customers exactly what you want them to do. In fact, the clearer your command, the less confusion there will be about the next steps. If possible, you can also include some type of offer or freebie. Very few customers would resist the opportunity to get a discount!

CHAPTER 5

Take a Deep Dive into Digital Marketing

**Every trackable interaction creates a data-point, and every data-point
tells a piece of the customer's story.**
Paul Roetzer

An Overview of Digital Marketing

Digital marketing is a type of marketing that is designed to appear on
electronic devices, such as mobile phones, tablets, computers, and other
devices. What makes it different from other forms of marketing, like
traditional marketing, is that marketers need to consider how to capture
the attention of audiences while they are online. This isn't as easy as you
may think because the average consumer sees about 6,000 to 10,000 ads
every day (Carr, 2021).

As a growing business, it is important to make your mark in the digital
world and build a recognizable brand that customers seek to follow and
support. You can do this by taking advantage of different digital
marketing tools to connect with members of your target audience. The
following sections will introduce you to some of the most effective tools
to promote and strengthen the presence of your business online.

Search Engine Optimization (SEO)

Search engine optimization (SEO) refers to the process of increasing
the visibility of your website through skillful use of keywords. The
higher your SEO ranking, the more "discoverable" your website will be
on search engines like Google. The main purpose of optimizing your

website is to attract more customers, or ensure that your business is amongst the top five choices whenever they are looking for a specific product or service.

Besides social media platforms, customers turn to search engines when searching for information. For instance, it is reported that Google receives 89.3 billion visitors on a monthly basis, and processes 8.5 billion searches per day (Mohsin, 2023). This means that search engines play a huge role in how customers get to know your business.

As a digital marketing strategy, SEO is also more sustainable than paid social media campaigns. In most cases, campaigns only last for a certain period, and when they end, so does the traffic going to your website. SEO, on the other hand, ensures continuous traffic, even when you aren't getting much from your social media pages. As a result, many businesses choose to invest in SEO in combination with other strategies like running social media ads or email marketing.

To get started with SEO, you will need to determine what exactly you would like to optimize. There are three types of SEO, all serving a different purpose, such as:

1. Technical SEO

Technical SEO allows you to optimize the technical elements of your website, such as your URL structure, navigation, and internal links. In other words, you are making your website pages or sections easily found on search engines. For example, if you would like customers to easily discover your homepage, you might use simple URLS like "About Amazon" or "What is Amazon" that match commonly searched keywords.

Other factors that affect technical SEO include how quickly your webpages load, mobile-friendliness, website security, and content management systems. In essence, the easier it is for search engines to understand and interpret your website data, the better your SEO ranking.

2. Content optimization

A popular type of SEO is content optimization. The reason why it is commonly used is because discoverable content not only boosts your website's ranking on search engine results, but it can also attract ideal customers. Optimizing content involves creating high-quality, targeted content that includes information that audiences are searching for. You can find out what audiences are searching for by Googling commonly used search engine keywords or topics.

Google will also reward websites for producing unique (i.e., original) and well-written content. This means that any plagiarism, imitation, or poorly written content won't be easily found on search engines. Other technical elements that can help you optimize content include title tags, header tags, image alt text, and meta descriptions.

3. Off-site optimization

Off-site optimization includes activities such as directing traffic from multiple online sources to your website. While this may not be SEO in the traditional sense, it can make your website more discoverable to audiences. A commonly used strategy for off-site optimization is link building. It involves strategically placing website links on third-party sites.

Please note that not every third-party site will generate traffic to your website. When choosing where to place your links, prioritize websites that are trusted, relevant, and frequently visited by your target audience. For instance, you might insert a website link on your social media pages and relevant blogs or forums that your customers visit. You can also consider promoting your website by creating eBooks, online courses, having a segment on a podcast, or creating YouTube videos.

A major part of successful SEO is analysis and reporting. If you don't measure your SEO efforts, you won't know how effective your content and website is in attracting customers. There are two ways to analyze SEO: website analytics and SEO tools.

Some websites, like WordPress-powered sites, come with complimentary website analytics dashboards that allow you to track and monitor the performance of your website. Additionally, you can create a Google Analytics account and integrate the code on your website to allow Google to track its performance too. SEO tools like Google Search Console, SEMRush, and KWFinder can help you search for common keywords and improve your site performance on search engines like Google.

It is also important to note that SEO needs constant updating. After all, what customers need or search for today may not be what they need or search for tomorrow. To keep your search engine ranking high, make sure that you update your content and constantly work on improving your website navigation, sophistication, and user experience.

Pay-Per-Click (PPC) Advertising

Pay-per-click (PPC) advertising is a form of digital marketing where you are charged every time an internet or social media user clicks on your post. In essence, you are paying each time someone engages with your content or follows a call-to-action (e.g., clicks on the "Buy now" button).

PPC ads are popular on search engines. They come in different sizes and formats, such as images, videos, or a combination of the two. They can also appear on social media platforms like Facebook, Instagram, Pinterest, TikTok, and LinkedIn, where they are targeted to specific types of users.

When PPC occurs over the internet, it is referred to as search engine advertising or marketing. Businesses place bids for ad placements on search engine results pages or on specific websites. When an internet user searches for related information, they are shown the sponsored business's link or advert.

Where and when your advert appears, as well as how much you pay for each click, depends on your budget, campaign settings (i.e., the size and characteristics of the people you want to reach), and the size of your ad.

This means that the higher the quality of your ad and bigger your budget, the better the placement and overall results of your PPC campaign.

Curating and inserting a good number of keywords will also affect how well your PPC ad performs on search engines and social media platforms. On sites like Google, for example, having relevant keywords can make your ad more discoverable to your audience. This is because your ad matches the type of information they commonly search for. It is therefore advised to do keyword research when designing your ad to increase engagement and traffic to your website.

Email Marketing

Did you know that email marketing is one of the most cost-effective and profitable direct marketing channels? It is estimated that for every $1 spent, you can make up to $42 (DMA, 2019). Due to the amazing return on investment, it is important to include this channel as part of your digital marketing strategy.

As the name suggests, email marketing allows you to share business content to a curated list of customers. Typically, this list is created based on the number of people who subscribe to receiving email correspondence from your business. This is perhaps one of the reasons why this form of communication is so effective—essentially, you are marketing to customers who voluntarily opt-in to receive information about updates, new product launches, promotions, and educational content.

When getting started with email marketing, the first step is to choose the right format. There are typically three types of email marketing, which are:

1. Promotional emails

Promotional emails are created to advertise special or limited-time offers, new product launches, complimentary discounts and codes, and exclusive products for premium customers (e.g., free eBooks or webinars for customers with a certain type of subscription/membership). Promotional emails tend to have a specific call-to-action that leads customers to a product page on the website or exclusive QR code or coupon.

2. Informational emails

Informational emails are created to share relevant business news, updates, and announcements to subscribed customers. A popular type of informational email is an e-newsletter, which is often sent once a month to share latest updates, milestones, or upcoming promotions and events. Another common type of informational email is an announcement. These are made less frequently than e-newsletters because they usually share information such as changes to service or customer policy, product launches, shipping delays, or technical glitches and faults.

3. Re-engagement emails

Another important type of email is the re-engagement email that is typically sent to get in touch with customers who haven't visited the website or made a purchase recently. It can also be sent to customers who abandoned their shopping carts and didn't follow through with making a purchase. The purpose of this email is to re-introduce your business, list the benefits of transacting with you, and offer an incentive to get customers to make a purchase. For instance, you can offer the customer a special discount code that they can use whenever they purchase a product within a specific time period.

While it is possible to send marketing emails through internet service providers (ISPs) like Gmail or Yahoo, it is not recommended. Not only does it tarnish the reputation of your business, it can also restrict you when it comes to sending hundreds of emails, or using professional templates. The better approach is to use bulk email service providers (ESPs) that come with the proper infrastructure and capacity to send mass emails, and provide analytics and reporting.

Fortunately, there are plenty of ESPs to choose from, some offering free plans and others charging a small monthly fee. Examples of the most popular ESPs in the market include:

- Mailchimp

- HubSpot

- Mailjet

- Constant Contact

When choosing the right provider, you will need to consider various things, such as how much you are willing to spend on an ESP per month, how many emails you plan to send, how many customers you will be emailing at a time, and your level of skill when designing emails (i.e., do you want an email you can customize, or one that is already designed for you?) If you are still growing your email list, and don't expect to send a lot of emails per month, then you can opt for a free plan. As your business grows and you require more features, a paid plan may be necessary.

Social Media Marketing

It is estimated that three-quarters of the world's population (aged 13 and older) are active social media users (Newberry, 2023). Social media platforms are the second-most visited place on the internet (the first being search engines like Google). This means that having a social media presence can increase brand awareness and help you get in front of the right customers.

Social media marketing is an umbrella term that describes the process of using social media to advertise your business. When most people hear "social media marketing," they think about PPC advertising; however, that is only one way of promoting your business on social media. Depending on your goals and objectives, you can build a community, collect user-generated content, or directly sell your products or services. Furthermore, when you aren't promoting your business, you can use social media for the following activities:

- **Content creation and planning:** social media gives you the opportunity to think about the best way to present your business. There are a variety of posts you can choose from—each with their specific advantages—which help you connect to audiences in a meaningful way, and build a captivating brand.

- **Social listening:** When you are conducting market research, you can access social media to gather information about your target audience, their activities, and the various topics they care about. Moreover, social media helps you keep an eye on your competitors and the various marketing campaigns they are pushing.

- **Social media analytics:** Social media platforms come with built-in analytical tools to help you measure the effectiveness of your posts and campaigns. They can also report on how much engagement your page is getting, and how users interact with your content.

- **Community management:** Another great benefit of social media is that you get to build a community and form meaningful relationships with customers. Instead of reaching out to you via email or contact forms on your website, customers can send you a message or leave a comment on your social media pages. Keeping your content unique, relevant, and aesthetically appealing can help you create ongoing engagement.

You may already be familiar with the various social media platforms available online, but did you know that each platform can be used to promote specific content? Below is a guideline of what to post on different social media platforms:

1. Facebook

Facebook is one of the biggest social media platforms on the internet, with over 2.9 billion users. With such a large audience, it is important to know what Facebook users are looking for so you can post engaging content. The platform is mostly used to connect with friends and family.

The types of content that often go viral on Facebook are those that provide value and entertainment. In terms of formats, videos have been found to receive higher engagement than images and links (Rayson, 2017). Examples of the types of videos you can post include how-tos, live videos, and blog post summaries.

2. Instagram

Instagram is an image-sharing social media platform that has over 1.3 billion users. Since the platform is built to share photos, the best type of content to post on Instagram are high-quality photos; however, in recent years Instagram stories and short-form videos have gained popularity. Examples of the kinds of visual content to post on Instagram include product photos, behind-the-scenes videos, and user-generated content (i.e., a photo of a customer holding your product or talking about your service).

3. TikTok

TikTok is a video-sharing social media platform that has over 1 billion users. Similar to Facebook, the type of content that goes viral is entertaining videos; however, the difference is that TikTok videos are typically 15 seconds or less. Examples of short-form videos users love to see include tutorials, product reviews, commentaries, skits or pranks, and influencer sponsorships.

4. Twitter

Twitter is a broadcasting social media platform that has over 450 million users. It is suitable for making announcements, launching new products, commenting about current affairs, and responding to customer queries or mentions. Text posts perform better than image or video posts on Twitter—plus, adding links has been found to increase the likelihood of "retweets" by 86% (Haltmeyer, 2022).

5. LinkedIn

LinkedIn is a professional networking social media platform, suitable for B2C and B2B marketing. The platform has over 134 million users who are there to look for job opportunities or expand their network. As a business, you can use LinkedIn to educate members of your target audience, search for talented staff, or share business developments and milestones. Custom images, infographics, and YouTube links have been found to increase post engagement and share rates.

Mobile Marketing

Mobile marketing is a fairly new type of digital marketing that was introduced in the early 2000s, around the same time that consumers started to transact and do business over their phones. The aim of mobile marketing is to distribute personalized mobile-friendly content or notifications, or location-sensitive information, over smartphones.

The type of content shown on mobile devices isn't necessarily unique to content shared on computer screens or tablets. The only difference is that on mobile devices, the content is often formatted and styled to look appropriate on mobile apps, text messages, and smaller smartphone screens. Nevertheless, mobile marketing strategies aren't the same as SEO or social media marketing strategies. Below are some of the most common and effective strategies to promote your business on smartphones:

1. App-based marketing

According to research, 80% of time spent on smartphones is spent on mobile apps, with mobile games taking up the largest share (Marrs, 2022). App-based marketing is about placing adverts, such as links or banners, in mobile apps. Services like Google Ad Mob help businesses create mobile-friendly ads that appear on various third-party apps. Facebook also helps businesses promote their ads on their custom mobile app, which appear on the target user's news feeds.

2. In-game mobile marketing

If you have identified members of your target audience who play mobile games, you can strategically place ads on third-party gaming apps.

Typically, they appear as banners, but they can also show up as full-page images or video ads that are inserted between loading screens (Marrs, 2022).

3. QR codes

QR codes are barcodes that are scanned by mobile device users that lead to specific landing pages. Businesses create and distribute QR codes to share more information about a particular product or pricing, access coupons and discounts, or to help customers complete a transaction.

4. Location-based marketing

Location-based marketing refers to ads that are shown to mobile devices based on their location. For example, you may want to show store promotions to customers within a specific radius from your physical store. Or you may want to send a notification to your customers whenever they drive to a specific location, like the office, gas station, or shopping mall.

5. Mobile search ads

If you would like your custom Google ads to appear on mobile devices, you can opt for mobile search ads. These ads look very similar to normal SEO marketing ads, except they include unique add-ons, like "show on maps" to help customers find your business location, "open in app" if your business has a profile on a specific mobile app, and "click to call" to copy the business phone number on the customer's dialing pad.

6. SMS marketing

Another unique mobile marketing strategy is SMS marketing. This type of advertising is only possible when you have access to your customers' cell phone number (i.e., when they opt-in to receive SMS notifications and updates). Using this format, you can send announcements, confirmations, and special offers through text message, with the option of inserting links.

The best way to assess which strategy works best with your customers is to test out as many as possible. You can also consider optimizing your ads to share information based on where your customers live or on third-party apps they frequently use.

With these five digital marketing strategies (SEO, PPC, email marketing, social media marketing, and mobile marketing), you have the tools to create and distribute high-quality content through digital channels, and build meaningful relationships with your customers!

CHAPTER 6

Branding and Brand Management

**If people like you, they will listen to you, but if they trust you, they'll
do business with you.**
Zig Ziglar

What Is Branding?

The American Marketing Association defines a brand as "a name, term,
design, symbol, or any other feature that identifies one seller's goods or
services as distinct from those of other sellers" (American Marketing
Association, n.d.). Before the 1950s, many businesses marketed
themselves as corporations, rather than brands. It was only when
companies like Procter & Gamble and Coca-Cola introduced elements
of branding, like having a distinct brand identity, that other companies
followed suit.

For Coca-Cola and Procter & Gamble, establishing a brand was for
strictly business purposes. They realized that the competition was
getting tougher, and the best way to distinguish their products from
competitors' products was to carry out what is now called "branding."
Branding is simply the process of giving significance to a business, or
its products and services, so that it can be memorable in the consumer's
mind.

How these two corporations built their brands was to focus on the
functional benefits of their products. For example, they would advertise
their products as being reliable, sophisticated, and of the highest quality.
By using these words: "reliable," "sophisticated," and "highest quality,"

they were able to position their products as being the best in their categories—and could therefore charge a higher price for them.

A few decades later, many other businesses had caught on. Building a brand became a way for companies to attract and retain customers, as well as to gain a significant market share. It was now common for a business to introduce itself through the brand, instead of through its corporate identity.

Depending on who the target audience was, and what their needs and values were, businesses were able to establish brands that were motivational, health-conscious, romantic, playful, or adventurous. No longer were brands just about distinguishing one company's products or services from another, but they also focused on selling a unique experience or way of life. Very quickly, businesses realized that they could affect how customers felt and the buying decisions they made by concentrating on building a strong brand.

Even companies who sold products that were socially seen as taboo could create a positive image in the minds of customers through skillful branding. A good example of this was a popular campaign by the cigarette brand Marlboro, owned by the tobacco company Philip Morris International Inc. It was created during a time when information about the dangers of smoking was released to the US public, and cigarettes got a bad reputation.

Instead of presenting counter-arguments to justify smoking, Marlboro decided to skillfully associate smoking with status. Their campaign introduced consumers to a character known as the "Marlboro Man," who symbolized independence and individualism. He was a macho man, who smoked Marlboro cigarettes while doing typical masculine tasks of that era, such as riding horses or fixing cars. He had a mind of his own; was a leader in his own right, and represented everything that a man at that time desired to be.

The campaign was a success because it motivated countless men to buy Marlboro cigarettes. It is reported that within a year, Marlboro cigarettes went from having 1% market share to being the fourth-largest cigarette brand in the world.

Creating a brand is an important milestone in marketing your business. You have the freedom to create an identity that both represents what your organization stands for, as well as what customers can resonate with. Your brand will be essentially what customers interact with on a regular basis; therefore, it is worth thinking about various components of building a strong brand. This chapter will introduce you to the main components of a brand, as well as the best practices when it comes to managing your brand.

The Face of Your Brand

What makes someone unique is their personal identity that cannot be replicated by anyone else. They might have a particular way of dressing, talking, or relating to others. The same applies with a brand. Each brand should have a unique brand identity that distinguishes it from other brands. When customers come across the brand's content online, they should be able to immediately recognize it.

A brand identity can be defined as the combination of elements that help a brand make a positive lasting impression. What makes the brand identity different from the brand image is that the latter is outside of the business's control. The public creates and manages the perception of a brand, but the brand identity—what the brand stands for and how it desires to be portrayed—is owned by the business.

Therefore, the first step in building a strong brand identity is to know who you are as a brand. You can explore more about who you are by answering the following questions:

1. Brand mission: What is your reason to exist as a brand? What gap do you hope to fill in the consumer's life?

_____

_____

_____

_____

_____

2. Brand values: What are your guiding principles as a brand? What are your beliefs and worldview?

_____

_____

_____

_____

_____

3. Brand personality: What human qualities does your brand have? If you had to build a persona, how would you describe yourself?

_____

_____

_____

_____

_____

4. Brand voice: What is your communication style as a brand? What tone of voice and language do you use?

_____

_____

_____

_____

_____

You are welcome to do research on existing brands and see how they have built their mission, values, personality, and voice to come through in their marketing.

The second component of building a brand identity is crafting a unique brand design. In order to stand out, your brand must look different. This means having distinct colors, symbols, and typography. Brand design includes corporate assets like your logo, product packaging, stationery, website design, and social media graphics and layouts. You can choose whatever fonts, color palettes, or images you believe best represent your brand; however, be mindful of how each design element complements each other and looks holistically.

In other words, choose fonts, colors, symbols, or images that don't clash or send opposing messages. It is also worth doing research on what kind of message fonts and colors communicate. For example, a classic font like Times New Roman is associated with tradition and trustworthiness. It is mostly used for brands that desire to be seen as credible, such as news publications or research institutions. Another example is the symbolism behind colors. A color like yellow represents playfulness and happiness, which is appropriate for a fun brand like McDonald's.

Once you have decided on all of your design elements, you can create a brand style guide, which is a document that outlines what elements to use, how to use them in different content pieces, and how often. Having a style guide will ensure that regardless of who manages your brand, they are all working from one blueprint.

Identify Your Brand Positioning

Brand positioning is another important component of building a strong brand. Earlier on, in Chapter 3, we discussed the importance of having a UVP, which is a statement that distinguishes one business from another, and highlights the benefits of its products or services. Brand positioning is similar, but has a different purpose to the UVP.

The purpose of brand positioning is to help you decide how you would like your brand to be seen by customers. It is about highlighting the significance of your brand—not necessarily your business or offerings—and why customers should trust you. The advantage of brand positioning is that it differentiates your brand from competitors without needing to make comparisons. All that is required is to be confident about what you know that you do best.

When deciding on your brand positioning, there are a few strategies to consider, such as:

1. Customer service positioning

If you are a customer-centric brand that has invested heavily on offering convenience to customers, then you might focus on customer service when positioning yourself. Highlight some of the systems you have implemented to increase response times and ensure exceptional service delivery. For example, do you have a 24/7 friendly support staff?

2. Convenience-based positioning

Most technological brands, including online businesses, may prioritize convenience above everything else. Doing business with these brands is simple, quick, and effortless. If you want to sell convenience, highlight processes that your business has simplified. For example, do you offer same-day or overnight deliveries? Or a flexible, stress-free return policy?

3. Price-based positioning

Some brands build their identity on the price of goods or services. For instance, Walmart's brand has been built around affordability and saving money. As such, they are able to attract customers who are budget-conscious. The risks of using this strategy are that, due to economic pressures, your price of goods or services may change, or that offering such low prices can create price wars with competitors.

4. Value-based positioning

Some customers purchase goods or services not because of the price, but the value that is associated with the goods or services. A luxury brand like Rolex sells the value and prestige of their watches, which allows them to put a price tag upwards of $10,000 for a timepiece. Another brand like Apple sells innovation and technology when promoting their devices to customers. Think about the value associated with your offerings. What are the intangible or emotional benefits that customers are given?

5. Innovation-based positioning

Not many brands will make use of this type of strategy because it requires you to be the first business to introduce a specific product or service in the market. Technology-based businesses like Apple or Tesla that have either invented or re-invented goods or services can make innovation their main selling point. The advantage is that they are guaranteed customers who are passionate about technology and innovation. Plus, being the first brand of its kinds creates prestige around the brand.

When crafting your brand positioning statement, you can follow the same steps as when you created a UVP. Continue to refine your statement until you believe it clearly defines who you are as a brand.

Craft Your Brand Messages

Once you have built a brand identity and defined your positioning, the only thing left to do is craft unique brand messages that communicate who you are and what you are all about. Without effective brand communication, you will find it difficult to attract the right customers or convey what makes you different.

Whether you would like the bulk of your communication to be online or in-person, your brand will need to use its voice through streamlined brand messages. You can think of brand messages as custom scripts that you have created to inform the tone, style, and language used when communicating to customers.

These scripts are influenced by your brand identity, particularly your values and personality. Therefore, whether you are sending an email or replying to a customer's comment on your social media page, how you communicate should sound the same.

A good example is the automobile company BMW that positioned its brand as the "ultimate driving machine" amongst competitors. Their mission has always been about delivering high-performing cars with uncompromised engineering. While their campaigns don't look the same, the brand messaging is always consistent. For instance, in one campaign they pushed forward the message "Some fear change, others drive it" and in another, "Passion wins." Both of these messages speak to the excellent craftsmanship and one-of-a-kind driving experience that BMW customers can expect (Marshall Strategy, n.d.).

When crafting your brand message, it is important to remember that your brand mission and positioning must be echoed in every content piece or communication channel where your brand exists, such as your website, blogs, social media pages, emails, company documents, and product packaging. Furthermore, the phrasing and language that you use must reflect your values, and be consistent throughout your channels. You will also need to regularly assess the effectiveness of your messaging, and ask yourself:

- Do our messages appeal to our target audience?

- Do our messages echo our brand positioning?

- Do our messages demonstrate our values?

- Are our messages consistent throughout our communication channels?

Your brand messages can be tweaked to remain relevant to your brand. A good exercise to practice when learning how to create content that sounds like your brand is to write about different topics using your brand's voice.

What Is Brand Management?

To ensure that your brand is sustainable in the long-term, you will need to find ways of maintaining your identity and reputation online and offline. The reality is that a single campaign won't be able to reach all of the members of your target audience, nor will a few articles or videos have posted on your website or social media pages. When you think about building your brand, you need to plan for the future and determine what needs to be done on a regular basis to promote your brand.

The simple definition of brand management is strategies that are implemented to continue increasing awareness and enhancing the value of your brand in customers' minds. Both startup and existing businesses should be focusing on brand management because every advertisement, campaign, or milestone counts in strengthening the perceived value of a brand.

Brand management strategies emphasize the following important factors:

- **Awareness:** To build a strong brand, members of your target audience need to know who you are and how you can positively impact their lives. Brand management focuses on increasing awareness through producing and sharing unique content.

- **Equity:** From the moment people find out about your brand, they are making assumptions about what kind of a business you are, and how much value you offer. To increase equity, leave no room for guessing, but instead sell your unique proposition and provide proof about why they should support your brand.

- **Loyalty:** Delivering on what you promised and investing in world-class customer service is what keeps customers happy and returning to your business. It is also what promotes brand loyalty, where customers decide to only come to you when seeking certain goods, services, or information.

- **Recognition:** When you have done the work to produce content aligned with your brand, customers will be able to recognize you online or offline through elements like your logo, colors, symbols, unique personality, or brand messages. Brand recognition is what fosters the other factors like increased awareness, equity, and loyalty.

- **Reputation:** Although your brand image is out of your control, you can monitor and listen to what customers think about you, and find ways to improve your reputation. This may include making decisions like asking existing customers to submit reviews, implementing more user-generated content into your marketing strategy, and showing proof of the quality of your products, or that you are upholding your brand values.

Besides being recognizable and developing a good reputation, effective brand management also helps you gain credibility. Depending on the specific products or services you offer, credibility can be the make-or-break factor of your brand.

For instance, if you are a vehicle manufacturer, customers are concerned about the quality of your engineering. The last thing a potential customer wants to read about is an engine fault that has been found in some of your vehicles. The same applies if you are a brand in the food industry; no customer wants to doubt the quality and freshness of your food. Brand management is what protects you from negative publicity and associations that could potentially ruin your brand.

On a regular basis, keep a watch on your online reputation. A simple and free way to do this is by searching for your brand or company name on search engine results pages. Look to see which sites mention your name, and what is said about you. If you detect your name on sites that are unknown, do some investigation. You may have agreed to the sharing of your contact and business information when signing on to a third-party platform.

Additionally, look for negative articles, comments, or reviews that have been written about you, and be proactive in getting in front of the narrative. If the article or review is true, own your mistake, be transparent about where the issue was, and provide an immediate solution (if possible). You can also take the complaint off the review channel by asking the customer to contact your customer service center. If you believe that an article, comment, or review was written maliciously, don't respond. Instead, report the site or user and shift your focus back on the things you can control.

Lastly, it is worth noting that brand management isn't a miracle cure to bolster your brand reputation. Your brand management strategies are only meant to help you maintain the positive work you are doing on a continuous basis to promote your brand. If you aren't doing the work, then no amount of reputation management will save you from complaints. Therefore, to build the kind of community and loyalty that boosts your brand, invest in the complete process of brand building.

CHAPTER 7

Marketing Automation

Marketing automation is the technology that propels your business into a new era of relationship-based marketing with quantifiable results.
Jon Miller

An Overview of Marketing Automation

Digital marketing involves carrying out a number of tasks, such as content planning, creation, scheduling, monitoring, and analyzing. These tasks are often repetitive and can be time-consuming. Marketing automation is the process of using software to complete some of the marketing tasks for you. Not only does this save you time, it can also increase the quality of output and ensure that you maintain the same look and feel of your brand over the long-term.

Many business owners are afraid of using marketing automation because it sounds like a complicated process. But the truth is that many businesses already use marketing automation without even knowing it. For example, if you have ever scheduled social media posts to go "live" on a certain date or used email service providers to send bulk emails to your subscribers, then you have experience with marketing automation.

Modern digital platforms have been upgraded to include some element of marketing automation to offer businesses like yours more convenience. If you are currently growing your business, but would like to focus your attention on other important tasks, then you can find ways to automate some of your repetitive marketing processes.

The good news is that automation software is user-friendly and typically designed to carry out a number of marketing tasks. This means that you won't need to pay for, and manage, multiple software. From a single dashboard, you can consolidate your marketing efforts, track the customer journey, build customer relationships, and prepare website and social media reports.

Benefits of Marketing Automation

You don't need to be a large business to benefit from marketing automation. Startups and small to medium-sized businesses can find value in integrating automation tools and software as part of their business processes. Below is a list of benefits of embracing automation:

1. Use your time more efficiently

When you aren't busy manually tracking or scheduling, you can spend more time refining your marketing strategy, and making sure that you are reaching your objectives. Furthermore, the beauty about software is that it is programmed to complete a series of tasks, at a professional standard, in a fraction of the time. If you are a new business that is still testing various marketing tactics, then automation can help you reach results a lot quicker.

2. Get a better understanding of your customers

When you have a computer that is monitoring and measuring your marketing initiatives on an ongoing basis, you will be able to get a more detailed picture of your ideal customer, and what challenges you can help them solve. Moreover, you can track the trends that emerge from your content, and see what kinds of posts or promotions have higher customer engagement.

3. Automate replies and follow-ups

Can you imagine how much time it would take to make the same formal introduction to 20 customers per day? Or respond to the same kinds of queries over and over again? Automation software allows you to customize frequent responses and follow-ups, so that you don't lose the essence of your brand's voice when engaging with different stakeholders (i.e., prospective customers, existing customers, employees, suppliers, and potential investors).

4. Predict future goals and budgets with more accuracy

When you are able to create and track a range of campaigns, analyze different metrics, and effectively calculate your ROI, it becomes easier to set more achievable objectives and budget for future marketing initiatives. You will save money by investing more into specific areas of your business where you have identified a lack, such as customer support or solidifying your brand identity.

5. Improve customer retention

Marketing automation software helps you manage the customer sales journey, and ensure that at each stage, customers are given the necessary information and incentives to proceed to the next stage. Software also helps you run loyalty programs, follow up with customers who have disappeared, respond to customer questions and messages from a single dashboard, and target specific customers for promotions. All of these strategies help to strengthen relationships with your customers and keep them coming back to your business.

Automating the Marketing Process

You might be wondering just how many of your tasks you can automate. In general, any task that you once performed on an Excel spreadsheet, or that you repeated in the same manner, more than once, is suitable for automation. Of course, you will still need to hire marketing personnel to perform tasks that cannot be replicated by a computer, like formulating a marketing strategy, but other "process" work can be done with software.

Below is a list of marketing activities that work well with automation.

Note that there are tools and software in the market that can manage these functions for you (more on this in the following section):

1. Lead tracking

It is difficult, if not impossible to follow up with every prospective customer that your marketing efforts reach, or that visit your website. Having a customer relationship management (CRM) system helps you track and manage interactions with existing and potential customers. For example, when they first enter your website, you can integrate a pop-up call-to-action to subscribe to your mailing list, or if they are seeking more information, you can direct them to your contact form. Thereafter, you are able to send custom, targeted emails, and nurture relationships on a long-term basis.

2. Social media marketing

According to a survey done by Sprout Social, 74% of consumers believe that brands should be posting an average of 1–2 times a day (Hill, 2022). Realistically, as a business owner, you won't always have time to create content, draft captions, and measure the effectiveness of your posts on a daily basis. A social media management software can help you create, schedule, post, and track the performance of your content on social media.

3. Website optimization

If you are running an online business, or tend to direct your customers to your website as one of the first contact points, automation can help you improve the user experience. For instance, you can integrate plugins to assist with easy navigation of your website, chatbots to help visitors who may have questions, and prompts that appear to help visitors complete an action. With each plugin you integrate, you can monitor the activities of site visitors, but of course, you will need to get their consent to collect this kind of data.

4. Content marketing

Not every business owner is good with words. If you don't have natural writing skills, you can use AI technology to create compelling content pieces. With new AI tools like ChatGPT, you won't need to spend a lot of time curating written content like captions, advert scripts, or articles. It is reported that AI writing software can produce over 2,000 blog articles in less than 15 minutes. This software also come in handy when generating scripted emails for your email marketing campaigns.

5. E-commerce marketing

If you are running an online store, you will need to guide customers through the process of buying, similar to how you would facilitate an in-person transaction. E-commerce marketing automation software can help you create and send beautifully designed invoices, integrate online payment services on your website, apply discount codes at checkout, calculate and schedule shipping, and so much more. Each step is triggered after the completion of the previous one, and a useful chatbot is available if customers have questions throughout the buying process.

Now that you are familiar with the types of marketing tasks you can automate, below are a few tools and software available for download online.

Popular Tools and Software

Did you know that about 56% of businesses use technology as part of their everyday operations? If you haven't yet embraced technology in your business, the best place to start is to automate some repetitive marketing tasks.

If you search for marketing tools and software on the internet, you will be overwhelmed with the amount of choice. There are so many new tools and software that are being tested and launched each day that picking the right ones becomes difficult. Here are a few tips that can help you assess the tools and software that are right for you:

1. Determine your marketing needs

A newly founded company will have very different marketing needs than a well-established medium-to-large business. Assess what your needs are based on the size of your business, type of business (i.e., industry, B2B/B2C, etc.), marketing goals, and number of customers you serve, so you can find a tool that provides the functions suitable for you.

2. Consider how tech-savvy you are

If you are going to be operating the tools or software on behalf of your business, then you will need to ensure that you are comfortable using the various tech services and platforms. There are tools, for example, that do most of the work for you (e.g., email marketing services with a "drag and drop" template feature), which means you don't need to have a high level of skill navigating them. Others are more sophisticated and require you to have some level of skill to get the most out of the tool.

3. Decide if you would like reporting options

Not every tool or software comes built with an analytical and reporting feature. If this is an important feature you need to run your marketing campaigns successfully, then be sure to include it in your list of criteria. If you are a small business, you may want to focus on establishing a presence and following online before you start to take metrics seriously. Tools or software that offer reporting can be an upgrade once you have connected to members of your target audience and are ready to start driving campaigns.

4. Stick to your budget

When you search for tools and software online, you will find both free and paid plan options. Free tools provide you with features that can help you complete basic tasks, but won't come with any add-ons or custom features. A free tool may also limit the number of customers you can target, data you can store, how many downloads you can make, or the quality of content you can produce. If you are testing a tool for the first time, start off with a free version, then upgrade your plan once you are ready to commit.

5. Request a free demo

Another useful tip is to request a demo, if the tool or software offers one. What's great about demos is that they give you a good indication of what the day-to-day management of the software will be like. While playing with the demo, you may discover limitations, such as difficulty navigating the software, or certain tasks that were not included. This will help you determine whether the software meets your needs.

To simplify your decision-making, here are a few popular marketing automation tools or software that can improve the running of your business:

Social Media Marketing

You can boost your engagement on social media by simply having the right tools at your disposal. Below are a variety of social media marketing tools that can help you streamline your marketing efforts:

1. Meta Business Suite

Meta Business Suite is a social media management and scheduling tool that is built into the Meta (previously known as Facebook) platform. It is free to use if you have a Facebook or Instagram business page or account, and can help you schedule posts, adverts, and stories on their mobile app or desktop version.

2. Hootsuite

Another great social media management and scheduling tool is Hootsuite. What's great about this tool is that it can monitor any of your social media pages and help you assess the performance of your marketing initiatives at a glance. You also have the ability to search for specific keywords, hashtags, locations, and mentions, and the tool will show you the trends and conversations that your target audience or competitors are engaging with. Downloading and using Hootsuite is free, but to access custom features you will need to upgrade your plan.

3. Buffer

Buffer is a social media analytical tool that can help you measure the performance of your social media content or pages. You can decide which metrics and platforms to focus on, and easily generate your own reports. Buffer also offers free content posting recommendations to improve your marketing effectiveness. The tool comes with a free 14-day trial, and thereafter charges $5 per month.

4. Lately and Hootsuite

Two companies, Lately and Hootsuite, have collaborated to provide business owners one of the best AI content generation tools, based on key metrics from your social media accounts. The tool first analyzes which keywords and phrases help you get the most engagement from your posts, and thereafter produces unique short and longform content that matches your brand's tone and voice. Moreover, the tool can take existing longform content, like blog articles, and break them down into various headlines or shorter captions that can maximize the performance of your ads and posts. Since the tool is powered by AI, it continues to refine the pool of keywords and phrases it uses to create content.

Email Marketing

It doesn't have to take you hours to create and send emails to your customers. There are multiple email marketing tools that can help you generate scripts, create customer segments or targeted mailing lists, and analyze how your email marketing campaigns perform (e.g., how many customers redeemed the offer made). Below are a few tools to consider:

1. Sender

Sender is one of the most popular free email marketing tools available in the market that helps you create beautiful newsletters using their easy "drag and drop" feature. The tool comes with hundreds of templates and fonts to choose from, and even allows you to customize email templates for each recipient. The built-in analytical tool shows you how many customers opened the email and followed the call-to-action links. The free plan lets you send 15,000 emails per month, to a maximum of 2,500 subscribers.

2. Omnisend

If you are operating an online small or medium-sized business, Omni send helps you send automated emails based on behavioral triggers, such as when a customer successfully completes a transaction. There are a range of email templates to choose from, including templates that allow you to advertise multiple products at once. It also offers a feature to send discount codes and gift boxes to increase engagement.

3. MailChimp

Another popular email marketing tool is MailChimp. On their free plan, you are able to create and schedule responsive emails, and use its recommendations feature to optimize your marketing campaigns. MailChimp also gives you the option to customize automated emails for each stage of the sales journey, such as welcome emails, abandoned cart reminders, and transaction confirmations.

Customer Relationship Management

According to Insider Intelligence, 60% of internet users cite bad customer service as one of the reasons they are hesitant to make online purchases (Lebow, 2021). Whether you run an e-commerce business or not, statistics like this show just how important it is to respond to customer messages and monitor conversations about your business online. The following CRM tools will help you manage communication with customers, in one comprehensive platform:

1. Zoho

Zoho is one of the best CRM tools for lead management. The tool helps you attract prospective customers and guide them through the sales journey, until they make a purchase. One of the ways that you can capture leads' information and contact details is through webforms. You can then interact with your leads through crafted email campaigns. The free plan is designed for one user only, who manages one pipeline and is able to capture and store 500 lead records. The paid options give access to multiple users, who manage three pipelines and can store more than 50,000 records.

2. Zendesk Sell

If you want to boost your conversion rate, then you can try Zendesk Sell. What is great about this tool is the amount of personalization it offers. For instance, you can create filtered lists of leads who are at a particular stage in the sales journey and craft emails to get them to the next stage. Additionally, Zendesk Sell's pipeline report shows you at which stage of the journey many leads are stuck, as well as through which digital channels leads engage with your brand. Using this information, you can identify where the problem lies and refine your marketing strategy. A free trial is available if you would like to play around with the tool, although plans start from $19 per month.

3. Intercom

Intercom boosts customer engagement by helping you form conversational relationships. This is done through integrating a chatbot on your website. You can program the chatbot to greet website visitors, respond to FAQs, capture emails, or leave personalized messages that encourage engagement. Prices for small businesses start from $79 per month and include website or app messaging, targeted outbound emails, and business and customer behavioral reporting.

CHAPTER 8

Hiring Marketing Personnel

Your talent determines what you can do. Your motivation determines how much you are willing to do. Your attitude determines how well you do it.
Lou Holtz

Signs It's Time to Hire a Marketer

It is common for a small business to start out with no marketing team. The business owner may be the person responsible for creating the marketing strategy and carrying out marketing tasks, until there comes a point where he or she cannot manage the tasks on their own.

Marketing automation only works with repetitive tasks that can be performed by a computer. The rest of the marketing tasks that require human intelligence, such as creating and overseeing the marketing strategy or building and maintaining an online community, need to be done by professional marketing personnel.

To buy time and save more on costs, you can find freelancers on platforms like Upwork or Fiverr who are able to perform these functions for you, but eventually, paying freelancers to manage marketing units or take on important functions in your company will start to become expensive too. This is usually when hiring experts to join your team is the most affordable and logical move.

Below are three telltale signs that your business is ready for an in-house marketing team:

1. **You are spending thousands of dollars hiring freelancers on a monthly basis.**

Hiring one freelancer to do an odd job won't cost you much. However, as soon as you hire more than one freelancer to perform tasks on an ongoing basis, this can become more expensive than hiring permanent or part-time staff.

2. **You have great ideas for your business but don't have the skill to compile a strategy.**

Leaders are naturally creative, but that doesn't mean that every leader knows how to compile a marketing strategy. They may have a strong vision for the company but need assistance from a professional marketer to craft a vision for their marketing initiatives, and align the goals and objectives with the brand and content produced.

3. **Your business growth is limited by the lack of brand initiatives.**

A trained and experienced marketer will understand things like how to build an effective brand or how to increase customer engagement. You may have reached the stage in your business where the lack of monitoring and measuring of your marketing efforts is affecting your potential revenue. In this case, it would be more profitable to pay someone who can optimize your marketing efforts and increase business revenue than continuing to get by on your own.

What Type of Marketing Professionals Do You Need?

Once you have made a decision to hire professional marketers, the next step is to determine what type of marketers you need, and in what capacity (i.e., part-time, full-time, etc.). Before you start the recruitment process, take a moment to reflect on the following questions:

- What are your current business goals? How do you envision marketing helping you achieve them?

- What do you imagine your marketer doing on a day-to-day basis? What duties would they handle?

- Are you looking for a marketing leader or someone to handle the daily marketing operations? Note that it takes two people to handle strategy and execution.

- Are you looking for people to join your team on a full-time or part-time basis?

- What kinds of skills do you believe your marketing team should have?

One of the common issues amongst small business owners is to hire one person (usually someone with 0–3 years of experience) who takes care of all the marketing duties. Although this is done to save costs, it can be detrimental to the business. It is important to remember that each type of marketer has been trained to perform a specific role. A strategist, for example, is trained to perform high-level planning and research to create achievable goals and objectives. On the other hand, a coordinator is trained to manage and oversee existing marketing channels and brand assets, and ensure they align with the set goals and objectives. Therefore, it is not feasible to have one person who wears both hats.

Here are examples of five different marketers and their respective roles:

Marketing Director

A marketing director performs marketing duties at an executive level. Their role requires them to oversee the marketing strategy of the business. Not only can they assess what customers need, they can create and manage marketing budgets, serve as a project or campaign manager, lead a team of junior marketers, and work with other departments to ensure that all marketing initiatives align with business goals.

Data Analyst

Collecting and analyzing data is an integral part of marketing success. While there is software that offer reporting, you may want someone whose role is to perform in-depth research and analysis on several aspects of the business, such as the target audience, competitors, industry trends and patterns, and so on. The data and insights gathered by the data analyst can inform several components of your marketing plan and strategy, such as how you position your business, the goals and objectives you set, and identifying the right marketing mix. As new data becomes available, the analyst will continue to collect, process, draw patterns, and even create models and algorithms.

Graphic Designer

A graphic designer is skilled in producing high-quality, unique visual content and elements. They can help you design a brand identity and manage the look and feel of your brand across all channels. Moreover, the graphic designer is responsible for creating visual content that is placed in social media adverts, blogs, websites, and product packaging. They can also work with other departments to coordinate visual elements on presentation slides, reports, mockups, etc.

Content Manager

The main function of a content manager is to maintain consistency in how the business communicates with internal and external stakeholders. Their role may include an element of public relations (PR), since they are responsible for managing the reputation of the brand. The position also requires strategy, planning, and coordination between the business's various communication channels.

SEO Strategist

SEO is such an important aspect of marketing that some businesses hire someone whose job is to take care of keyword research, identifying the best call-to-actions (and where to place them), optimizing website content, and analyzing top competitors and their content strategies. In teams where there isn't anyone responsible for content creation, the SEO strategist will play the role of copywriter as well (however, they would only be in charge of writing SEO-rich content).

How Your Marketing Team Can Collaborate with Other Departments

"Collaboration" is one of those words that is mentioned over and over again during internal discussions. The reason why it is so important is that it ensures organizational success. Even though employees are grouped into specialty teams or departments, they are all working toward the same company vision and goals. Therefore, it is wonderful when teams find ways to work together on projects or include each other during brainstorming sessions because this is what improves the quality of outcomes.

Here are a few benefits of cross-functional collaboration:

- **Higher quality of work:** When teams work together, they are able to share skills and knowledge, and deliver projects that combine the expertise of several different people. The final outcome is likely to be of a higher caliber than if teams were working alone.

- **Improved problem-solving.** When teams brainstorm and solve problems together, there is a greater potential for innovative ideas to come forward. For example, one team that specializes in a particular function (e.g., finance) tends to bring a unique perspective that another team which specializes in a different function (e.g., marketing) cannot.

- **Enhanced company culture:** When teams feel comfortable collaborating and sharing the responsibility of making the company better, they are able to unite on common values and behave like a solid unit. This can positively impact employee engagement and lead to higher work satisfaction.

- **Gaining unique insights:** Every team or department within the organization is responsible for conducting research to perform their duties. When teams come together, they are able to share data and insights about customers, products, sales, or the logistics and distribution model of the business. Gaining unique data and insights can improve strategy and decision-making.

The good news is that the marketing team can collaborate with almost every team in the organization. However, there are four teams in particular that make a great collaboration, such as:

1. Marketing and sales team

Both these two teams are concerned about connecting with customers. The marketing team will focus on finding leads through promoting the brand and producing relevant content, while the sales team will focus on converting leads to paying and loyal customers. The marketing and sales teams have an opportunity to align on the process of acquiring customers and generating the right messages.

2. Marketing and support team

What the marketing and support team have in common is that they both care about enhancing the customers' experience. While the marketing team will focus more on creating that initial connection, the support team will nurture customer relationships in the long-term. The teams can work together to craft email and support messages that match the brand's tone and voice. They can also help each other respond to social media, website, or email queries, and escalate complaints before they become big.

3. Marketing and design team

These two teams can have a lot of fun collaborating on visual aspects of the brand. The marketing team will bring a clear and actionable brand strategy and the design team will create visual symbols, elements, and content to bring out the brand's personality. The teams can work together to ensure that the brand visuals are consistent throughout channels.

4. Marketing and product development team

Businesses that manufacture physical products will most likely have a product development team. They may be knowledgeable about building smart products, but won't always know what sells. The advantage of collaborating with the marketing team is that they can get fresh data and insight about customer pain points, or feedback about what customers are saying on social media about the product. Gaining this knowledge will assist the development team with testing and refining the product.

The Future of Marketing and Trends to Watch

With each year, there are new technologies being introduced that shift how we do business and interact with people. In recent years, we have been stunned by the development of AI tools and how they are able to simplify marketing processes and help us get quality results in a fraction of the time.

Even though no one can say with certainty what the future of marketing will look like, we can make predictions based on trends that are starting to develop now. Below are a few marketing trends that are growing in popularity:

1. Conversational marketing

Mobile marketing is fast becoming the preferred choice for brands to share their messages. However, since "chatting" on mobile devices is casual, marketers are having to adjust their approach when delivering messages. Conversational marketing is a new trend inspired by mobile marketing, which seeks to prompt one-on-one conversations with customers.

The aim is to integrate brands into customers' lives by humanizing them—making them sound and behave like real people. Conversational marketing is best practiced through live chat or chatbots, since this can easily create a personal brand experience.

2. Social media optimization

Above and beyond optimizing SEO, businesses are starting to optimize social media content. This is because they are finding that a large portion of people's time is spent online, thus providing an opportunity to connect with them in a more targeted and intentional way. It is becoming more common for data to be collected through social media monitoring, as well as through engaging and partnering with influential content creators and large social media communities.

3. Artificial Intelligence (AI)

"AI" has become the new buzzword in the marketing industry. Developers are creating more AI-powered tools to assist in content creation, automating tasks, and personalizing experiences with customers. In order to maximize the use of this technology, marketing teams need to educate themselves on how AI works, and how they can successfully integrate this tool into their marketing strategies.

4. Web3

The internet has evolved several times since its inception. When we were first introduced to the world wide web, engineers had built Web 1.0, which consisted of static web pages that displayed general news, specialist information, and interest-based blogs and business websites. As technology got smarter, Web 2.0 was introduced. Engineers were now able to make pages load more quickly, pull up hundreds of thousands of search results based on a few keywords, and create shareable images and videos.

Web 3.0 is the future of the internet that is based on open-source and decentralized data networks. Instead of data being stored in a centralized server, individuals and businesses will be able to build smaller online networks and create more personalized marketing experiences. For example, your brand can create virtual events, accept bitcoin as a form of payment, and embrace gamification by making customers earn points or tokens for constant engagement. Nevertheless, Web3 is still in development and many people are still speculating about how it will change the world of marketing.

Conclusion

Creativity may well be the last legal unfair competitive advantage we can take to run over the competition.
Dave Trott

Marketing and sales exist to help your business find customers who will most likely buy your products or services. However, to create a winning marketing strategy, you must look beyond revenue and profit margins, and consider different ways to build and nurture genuine relationships with your customers.

Realistically speaking, there will always be a company that sells products or services that are smarter, cheaper, and more appealing than yours. This is why selling the features of your offerings isn't enough to make customers choose to support your business. What you need to sell is an experience that is so unique that customers are forced to come to you whenever they need certain solutions.

In this book, we have discussed various sides of marketing and sales, from identifying your target audience to converting them into paying customers through skillful marketing tactics. The aim was to show you how to find and keep customers, long after they have made a sale.

While it is good to get customers to buy from you, it is important to think about the long-term marketing goal and objectives. In other words, after the customer has made a purchase, what then? What are the next steps? How can you continue the conversation and build a long-lasting relationship?

Needless to say, after reading this book, you have a lot of researching, brainstorming, and strategizing to do. But the good news is that you don't have to do all of the work alone. Automation tools and software can handle time-consuming and analytical tasks, while hired marketing professionals can help you build a powerful brand and community of engaged and loyal customers.

Continue to invest in learning about the marketing industry and the various technological trends that are changing the way businesses interact with customers. It may seem like a long time ago when you last read a newspaper ad—and this alone should show you how quickly the industry is evolving! What is current today may be considered "history" in a few years. Therefore, make an effort to stay up-to-date with trends making waves in the market.

If you have found this book valuable, please leave a review!

References

Activate Design. (n.d.). What's the difference - modern marketing vs traditional marketing. Www.activatedesign.co.nz. https://www.activatedesign.co.nz/Blog/modern-marketing-vs-traditional-marketing#:~:text=While%20traditional%20marketing

Akasa. (2022, February 8). 29 Of the best AI and automation quotes. Akasa. https://akasa.com/blog/automation-quotes/

American Marketing Association. (n.d.). Branding. American Marketing Association. https://www.ama.org/topics/branding/

Authentic Brand. (2021, February 23). When to hire a marketer and what type of marketer your business needs. Authentic Brand. https://authenticbrand.com/marketing/when-to-hire-a-marketer/

Baker, K. (2022, November 3). The ultimate list of marketing quotes for digital inspiration. Blog.hubspot.com. https://blog.hubspot.com/marketing/marketing-quotes

Barone, A. (2022, June 13). Marketing strategy. Investopedia. https://www.investopedia.com/terms/m/marketing-strategy.asp

Bennett, P. (2021, July 30). Marketing effectiveness: How to measure it and present to external stakeholders. Blog.hubspot.com. https://blog.hubspot.com/marketing/easy-ways-to-measure-the-effectiveness-of-your-content

Birkett, A. (2022, September 9). The 14 best marketing automation software tools available to you. Blog.hubspot.com. https://blog.hubspot.com/marketing/marketing-automation-software-tools

Capers, Z. (2021, March 22). Startups are adopting marketing technology in droves—But how effective are their stacks? GetApp. https://www.getapp.com/resources/marketing-technology-stack/?utm_source=sgrind&utm_medium=mediumblog

Carr, S. (2021, February 15). How many ads do we see a day in 2023? Lunio. https://lunio.ai/blog/strategy/how-many-ads-do-we-see-a-day/#:~:text=In%20the%2070s%2C%20the%20average

Chi, C. (2021, June 23). How to set and achieve marketing objectives in 2021. Blog.hubspot.com. https://blog.hubspot.com/marketing/marketing-objectives

Conlin, B. (2018). 5 Tech trends that will influence your marketing strategies. Business News Daily. https://www.businessnewsdaily.com/8564-future-of-marketing.html

deBara, D. (2017, July 31). What is brand identity? And how to design and develop a great one. 99designs; 99designs. https://99designs.com/blog/tips/brand-identity/

Demand Metric. (2019). Content marketing infographic. Demandmetric.com. https://www.demandmetric.com/content/content-marketing-infographic

DMA. (2019). Marketer email tracker 2019. DMA. https://dma.org.uk/uploads/misc/marketers-email-tracker-2019.pdf

Doxee. (2020, August 20). What is the marketing mix? From the original 4Ps to their evolution in 7Ps. Doxee. https://www.doxee.com/blog/marketing/what-is-marketing-mix-origins-evolution-in-the-digital-age/

Fanning, E. (2020, April 20). What is email marketing and how does it work? Sendinblue. https://www.sendinblue.com/blog/what-is-email-marketing/

Focus7. (2018, August 29). How to identify your marketing objectives. Focus7. https://focus7international.com/2018/08/29/how-to-identify-your-marketing-objectives/

Gesch, A. (2020, January 10). 22 Best branding quotes to inspire you. 99designs. https://99designs.com/blog/business/branding-quotes/

Godlash, F. (2015, April 28). 15 Tips on fixing your brand's bad reputation. Mediabistro. https://www.mediabistro.com/climb-the-ladder/managing/15-tips-fixing-brands-bad-reputation/

Goss, M. (2022, September 30). Top 5 trends for the future of marketing. SearchCustomerExperience. https://www.techtarget.com/searchcustomerexperience/feature/Top-5-trends-for-the-future-of-marketing

Great Content. (2019, December 16). Storytelling marketing 101 : Learn the magic techniques of storytelling in content marketing. Great Content. https://greatcontent.com/storytelling-in-content-marketing/

Haltmeyer, M. (2022, November 22). Tailoring social media content for different platforms. Blog.ironmarkusa.com. https://blog.ironmarkusa.com/utilize-social-platforms

Hanlon, A. (2022, January 11). How to use the 7Ps marketing mix? Smart Insights. https://www.smartinsights.com/marketing-planning/marketing-models/how-to-use-the-7ps-marketing-mix/

Hati, S. (2021, May 18). How Marlboro became the largest cigarette brand in the world. Sanket Communications. https://www.sanketcommunications.in/marlboro-man-the-magic-of-lifestyle-marketing/

Hill, C. (2022, August 25). How often to post on social media. Sprout Social. https://sproutsocial.com/insights/how-often-to-post-on-social-media/

Indeed. (n.d.). What is the definition of a marketing mix? Www.indeed.com. https://www.indeed.com/hire/c/info/marketing-mix

Indeed Editorial Team. (2022a, June 25). 20 Targeting questions to understand your target audience. Indeed Career Guide. https://www.indeed.com/career-advice/career-development/targeting-questions

Indeed Editorial Team. (2022b, June 25). Brand messaging framework: The 8-step guide to creating one. https://www.indeed.com/career-advice/career-development/brand-messaging-framework

Indeed Editorial Team. (2023, February 4). Brand management: Definition, examples and tips for success. Indeed Career Guide.

https://www.indeed.com/career-advice/career-development/brand-management

Keane, L. (2019, March 15). Target market segmentation: How to use it to your advantage. GWI. https://blog.gwi.com/marketing/target-market-segmentation/

Keap. (n.d.). What is marketing automation? Keap. https://keap.com/marketing/how-does-marketing-automation-for-small-business-work

Kim, L. (2019). What is PPC? Learn the basics of pay-per-click (PPC) marketing. Wordstream.com. https://www.wordstream.com/ppc

Kirsty. (2021, January 9). How marketing can work effectively with other teams in a business. ContentCal. https://www.contentcal.com/blog/how-marketing-work-effectively-other-teams-business/

Kuehlwein, J. P. (2016, September 1). A brief history of branding. Branding Strategy Insider. https://brandingstrategyinsider.com/a-brief-history-of-branding/

Lake, L. (2022, December 30). What is a target audience? The Balance. https://www.thebalancemoney.com/what-is-a-target-audience-2295567

Lebow, S. (2021, January 25). The customer is always right: The reason why 60% of internet users hesitate when shopping online. Insider Intelligence. https://www.insiderintelligence.com/content/customer-always-right-reason-why-60-of-internet-users-hesitate-shopping-online

Lua, A. (2017, September 7). What to post on Facebook, Instagram, Twitter, LinkedIn, and more. Buffer Library. https://buffer.com/library/what-to-post-on-each-social-media-platform/

Lytho. (2020, November 5). How to segment a target audience. Insights.lytho.com. https://insights.lytho.com/segment-target-audience

Mailchimp. (2021a). What is content marketing? Content marketing definition. Mailchimp. https://mailchimp.com/marketing-glossary/content-marketing/

Mailchimp. (2021b). What is digital marketing? A beginner's guide. Mailchimp. https://mailchimp.com/marketing-glossary/digital-marketing/

Marinaki, A. (2021, April 23). 80 Glorious marketing quotes to empower and inspire you. Moosend. https://moosend.com/blog/marketing-quotes/

Marion. (2015, October 27). What is branding? The Branding Journal. https://www.thebrandingjournal.com/2015/10/what-is-branding-definition/#brand-definition

Marrs, M. (2022, March 3). What is mobile marketing and why does it matter so much? Wordstream.com. https://www.wordstream.com/blog/ws/2013/08/19/what-is-mobile-marketing

Marshall Strategy. (n.d.). 5 Examples of strategic brand messaging. Marshall Strategy. https://www.marshallstrategy.com/our-services/messaging-strategy/brand-messaging-examples/

Mohsin, M. (2023, January 13). 10 Google search statistics you need to know in 2023. Www.oberlo.com. https://www.oberlo.com/blog/google-search-statistics#:~:text=Google%20is%20visited%2089.3%20billion%20times%20a%20month.

Moody, S. (2022, October 31). Prep your team for the future of marketing with these key lessons. Contently. https://contently.com/2022/10/31/future-of-marketing-will-change-the-team/#:~:text=The%20future%20of%20marketing%20is

Nag, P. (2022, February 22). 9 Boring marketing processes you should automate right now. Www.getresponse.com. https://www.getresponse.com/blog/marketing-processes-automate

Newberry, C. (2023, January 4). What is social media marketing? [complete 2023 guide]. Social Media Marketing & Management Dashboard. https://blog.hootsuite.com/social-media-marketing/

Nordqvist, C. (2018, November 11). What is a marketing strategy? Definition and examples. Market Business News; Market Business News. https://marketbusinessnews.com/financial-glossary/marketing-strategy/

Omniconvert. (2023, March 6). What is a UVP (unique value proposition)? Omniconvert. https://www.omniconvert.com/what-is/uvp-unique-value-proposition/

Patel, N. (2016, January 4). 5 Marketing processes you should seriously consider automating. Neil Patel. https://neilpatel.com/blog/marketing-processes-you-should-automate/

Patel, S. (2021). The 2019 guide to successful brand positioning in your market. Hubspot.com. https://blog.hubspot.com/sales/brand-positioning-strategy

Raeburn, A. (2022, June 15). Brand messaging 101: A complete guide. Asana. https://asana.com/resources/brand-messaging-framework

Rayson, S. (2017, August 29). Here's why brand and publisher Facebook engagement fell in 2017. BuzzSumo.com. https://buzzsumo.com/blog/facebook-engagement-brands-publishers-falls-20-2017/?ref=buffer-library

Rudder, A. (2022, March 21). The best marketing CRMs of 2022. Forbes Advisor. https://www.forbes.com/advisor/business/software/best-marketing-crm/

Salesforce. (n.d.). What is marketing automation? Salesforce.com. https://www.salesforce.com/eu/learning-centre/marketing/what-is-marketing-automation/

Search Engine Land. (2017). What is SEO/Search Engine Optimization? Search Engine Land. https://searchengineland.com/guide/what-is-seo

Skyword Staff. (2020, October 2). 365 Marketing quotes to keep you fired up all year. Skyword. https://www.skyword.com/contentstandard/marketing-quotes/

Square Australia. (2021, July 12). How to use the 7Ps of marketing in 2021. Square. https://squareup.com/au/en/townsquare/how-to-use-7ps-of-marketing

Zote, J. (2023, February 1). 7 Ways to tap into your true target audience. Sprout Social. https://sproutsocial.com/insights/target-audience/